Seeloomar

Heinemann Organization in Schools Series

General Editor: Michael Marland

Departmental Management

edited by

MICHAEL MARLAND

Headmaster
North Westminster Community School, London

and

SYDNEY HILL

Director of Studies
Christopher Wren School, London

with contributions by

COLIN BAYNE-JARDINE
RORY DEALE
COLIN HARRISON
MAURICE HOLT
ANN IRVING
GEORGE PHIPSON
and
PETER STOKES

HEINEMANN EDUCATIONAL BOOKS
LONDON

Heinemann Educational Books Ltd
22 Bedford Square, London WC1B 3HH

LONDON EDINBURGH MELBOURNE AUCKLAND
HONG KONG SINGAPORE KUALA LUMPUR NEW DELHI
IBADAN NAIROBI JOHANNESBURG
EXETER (NH) KINGSTON PORT OF SPAIN

Departmental management.- (Heinemann Organization in
Schools Series).
1. Departmental chairman (High schools) -
Great Britain
I. Marland, Michael   II. Hill, Sydney
373.12'013   LB2901

ISBN 0-435-80591-6

Typeset by The Castlefield Press of Northampton
in 11pt Baskerville, and printed in Great Britain by
Biddles Ltd, Guildford, Surrey

Contents

Acknowledgements

The substance of this book grew out of a series of in-service courses run at Churchill College, Cambridge, by Organization in Schools Courses. Our first thanks, therefore, are to those responsible for mounting the courses, and to the members of the courses, whose questions, examples and suggestions were most helpful.

MICHAEL MARLAND and SYDNEY HILL

Preface

The Heinemann Organization in Schools Series is a systematic attempt to help schools improve the quality of the secondary-school experience by a methodical study of the ways in which they can be organized and administered. The series has been planned to cover the central philosophy and every aspect of the planning and running of schools. Each book has been written by a different author and from a different point of view, out of his or her own observation, experience, and conviction. Some, like the present volume, have several contributors. There is inevitably some overlapping between volumes, as certain topics (such as the responsibilities of senior staff, or the provision of resources) need to be included in a number of books.

The first book to be published in the series was *Head of Department*,[1] reflecting the importance of that post in the comprehensive school and hoping to answer the need felt by thousands of teachers for help in preparing for and carrying out the tasks involved. The present book is a complementary one, continuing the exploration of the work in greater detail, but not repeating aspects covered in that book. Thus the first book discussed building a team, discussion methods, student teachers and parents — topics not covered in detail in the present book. On the other hand 'the subject' was covered only briefly there, and that introduction is complemented here by Part Three: "The Subject and the Skills". Both books can be read independently, but together they form a substantial outline of the head of department's work.

In the years during which this series, and its associated Organization in Schools Courses, has developed, the role has become more important and if anything more demanding.

[1] Michael Marland, *Head of Department* (Heinemann Educational Books, 1971).

Post-holders are now approaching it with a new professionalism, and I hope this volume will enhance that.

MICHAEL MARLAND

Introduction:
the tasks of a head of department
Michael Marland

'The success of a comprehensive school depends to a very great degree on the understanding of their jobs by the heads of departments.' That central fact of education in this country is as true now as when I wrote it in *Head of Department,*[1] the book related to this. It also remains true that there is little help available to the prospective or actual holder of these posts. It is clear that insufficient attention has been paid by researchers and students of educational administration, by providers of in-service training, and by those responsible for career development in schools, to the needs of heads of department. Their function is unique to this country, and is a clear, practical demonstration of the philosophy of the devolved system of educational responsibility in Britain.

The way this devolution of responsibility has affected the nature of the school is not fully appreciated. The key points can be summed up briefly:

1 The UK school is largely autonomous, and therefore its structure, procedures, curriculum and counselling can be devised within the school (that being so, it is remarkable how little difference there is between schools!)
2 The professional career structure and additional payments see promotion clearly as related to further *responsibility*
3 Administration and pedagogy are fused, quite unlike, for instance, the USA, in which headteachers are actually called 'administrators', belong to different unions, never teach, and have substantially different contracts
4 The head of department is regarded as a senior member of the overall leadership and planning of the school.

We should relish these aspects of our system, and be true to them by exploiting them fully. They have their obvious difficulties, but that is no reason for only half-heartedly responding to their strengths. Indeed, if we fail to do that,

[1] Heinemann Educational Books, 1971.

we risk having the worst of both worlds, and would be better with an education system that retains all significant power and decision-making outside the school!

As George Phipson and Colin Bayne-Jardine make clear (Chapters 2 and 3), the head of department requires intellectual, administrative and human relationship skills of a high order. His tasks are spelt out in the first book, and some of them are worked out in greater detail in this. He needs to:

1 Structure the departmental team, utilizing the flexibility of the responsibility post system to create a cogent internal structure
2 Take a major part in appointing teachers
3 Deploy teachers in a way which is consistent with their strengths and weaknesses and their career development — as well as fulfilling the needs of the school
4 Monitor teachers' work
5 Assist the development of teachers' professional skills, both as required by the school, and to assist their own growth for the future
6 Contribute to the initial training of student teachers on teaching practice
7 Take a part in the planning of the school's overall curriculum, and lead the planning of the curriculum within the department
8 Oversee the work of the pupils, from the monitoring of their progress, through disciplining and encouraging, to reporting
9 Manage the finances, physical resources, and learning materials efficiently
10 Assist in the overall leadership of the school.

To do this requires a range of abilities, but it also requires a clear understanding of the situation — in particular of the effects of delegation from the headteacher to the head of department and the particular difficulties created in schools by this role.

The effects of delegation

The word is used loosely in schools, indeed it is often confused with sheer laziness. What is less often analysed is what are the actual effects on the nature of a task when it is delegated — for the task itself changes.

In the 'simple', single-order school the head is *directly* responsible (under the articles of government and in consultation with governors) for 'the conduct and curriculum' of the school. In the large comprehensive school, facets of this responsibility are delegated to the head of department. This delegation has important advantages and disadvantages. A careful understanding of these helps to make the best of the situation. Only by realizing what is happening can the head of department produce complementary balances.

Let us compare, then, the head in, say, a two-form entry secondary modern school and the head of a large department on a similar salary in a large comprehensive school:

The advantages

1 The head of department is considerably more knowledge-able than the headteacher in the particular subject.
2 The head of department is likely to be considerably more active, initiating more.
3 The head of department can be closer to the individual teachers in the team, knowing them personally as well as professionally.

The disadvantages

1 Whereas the headteacher sees the whole range of learning, the head of department is inexorably pulled towards a single focus only: the subject. Much of the first three chapters of this book is devoted to facing this problem and trying to re-focus the head of department in a school context.
2 Although both headteacher and head of department are very busy, the head of department has considerably less *deployable* time. The head is only diary-bound; the head of department is firmly timetable-bound, and the first can be re-deployed, whereas the second cannot. This is a major constraint on the effectiveness of his task, and has very great significance for the mode of working. The job cannot be done by charisma alone or by constant personal inter-vention — system and careful responsibility structure are particularly required.
3 The third disadvantage is the corollary of being close. It is very difficult to be close to a team of teachers, indeed working as one of them and mixing with them as a complete equal, and yet exercise the objective judgement that the head of that small school used to be able to exercise. The good head of department naturally tries to get very, very close to his team. But then, when he turns round and actually has to find some way of assessing the work of one of the team, of judging that teacher, maybe

of criticizing, it is extraordinarily difficult, because that head of department has become so close and friendly. We are particularly bad at this in England. The Americans find it easier to be companionable and yet on occasions to have the functional distance to be critical. In this country, we tend to lose one when we gain the other. That makes the head of department's job very difficult indeed. It would be fair to say of many heads of department that their major fault is their unwillingness to say the hard things that sometimes need saying. I can think of an instance of a very good head of department who, when I asked for advice on drawing up a testimonial for one of his subordinates applying for another job, gave me some critical information about that subordinate. When I asked if he had told that subordinate, the head of department said, 'Well, no; he would be terribly upset!' I pointed out that he would be even more upset if the points went in a testimonial without his being told. It is a head of department's duty to say the unpleasant things that need saying, not merely to be so frightened of losing a friendship that he is not willing to make the criticism. One of the most difficult personality problems comes from this ambivalence between being close to your team and at the same time being able to stand back and say, 'I'm sorry, but . . .'. From the day you first take a Scale 2 post until the day you retire as a head-teacher, it is the hardest job of all to be able to say 'I'm sorry, but . . .' and yet retain friendship.

The difficulties of the job

Although working heads of departments are very sharply aware of the general difficulty of the job, the problems are usually left as an unanalysed burden. It is worth being more clear about what causes the difficulties, for then it is easier to take at least some steps towards solving them.

Overlapping teams

The writers in this book tend to talk, as I do myself, of 'the' departmental team. In fact, of course, no head of department has the sole allegiance of his team members. They will mostly be tutors (with allegiance to the head of year or house); many will also teach other subjects (with allegiance, therefore, to other heads of department); and all will have playground duties, extra-curricular activities, and non-departmental responsibilities, each with its own team leader. The clearer the sense of hierarchy in the school, the easier it is to cope with this: each person must be seen as belonging to the appropriate position for the main activity of the moment. It does mean, however, that a scheme or way of running a department must not depend on excessive calls on members' time. Some departmental discussion meetings, some Mode III examination marking, and certain styles of teaching requiring continuous material presentation, for instance, are possible only for the devoted full-time member of the team who has no other function. A rarity!

Acceptance

It is a difficult point of judgement, too often clouded by personal feelings about the people concerned, to know when to accept that something or somebody's way of acting cannot be changed and must be accepted. The general stance of this book is that most difficulties in a school can at least be worked on, and some steps taken towards their amelioration. Yet the head of department has to know when to take no for an answer, when to accept that something cannot be changed, or is not worth the effort of changing. Perhaps most important, the head of department has to be able to accept hierarchically appropriate decisions, even if they are ones which personally that head of department would not have made.

Criticism and praise

We all need appropriate praise and criticism. Peter Stokes argues (in Chapter 5) the importance of monitoring the teachers' work in the classroom. It can, however, be difficult to get the balance right. A bland sequence of praise, when some parts of a person's job are being carried out quite obviously poorly, is as bad as a constant carping when at least some things are going right.

Administration

It will be noticed that there is no section on administration in either *Head of Department* or the present book. This is deliberate; it is not a separate part of the job, but an aspect of every part of the job. Success requires a way of looking at matters which habitually works backwards from what is required, and *imaginatively* traces the necessary steps backwards to the deduced starting date — usually much earlier than expected. There is a very brief section on coping with paperwork in Appendix 1, but beyond that we have preferred to analyse the role by its aspects, rather than its methods, and administration belongs to every aspect of the head of department's work.

Finally, I wish to stress that the overall theme of this collection is the relationship between the department and the school. There is no way towards a coherent school that can grow out of the individual department run as 'a school within a school'.

PART ONE

Autonomy and Integration

The first three chapters consider the task of department management as part of the larger task of the school: how it influences, and is influenced by, general curricular issues; how it relates to the complex framework of school management and decision-making structures. Finally, a definition of good practice is put forward which refers to the issues above and touches on many others. The need for integration with other departments and with the school is stressed, as is the much cherished and easily abused autonomy that characterizes the English educational system, especially at management level.

1 The head of department and the whole curriculum

Maurice Holt

Any substantive statement about the curriculum is a statement about values. This is true of the title of this paper, for the assumption is that in defining the whole curriculum, it is not enough merely to define the separate departments which contribute to the learning experiences of the curriculum.

This assumption, however, is at odds with the traditional view of the secondary curriculum as a collection of separate subjects — a view which led directly to the notion of the head of department as a subject teacher exalted above his fellows in order to control all a school's work in a given subject. The clear implication is that the curriculum is made up of well-bounded subjects, and that a school's curriculum will be as effective as the sum of the separate subject contributions. This additive, rather than interactive, view of the curriculum was strongly associated with the grammar school, and reinforced by separate subject examinations at GCE O level and A level. Evidence to support the view that the head of department was chiefly concerned to do well for the ablest comes from Lacey's analysis[1] of how the teaching in a 1960s grammar school was allocated between staff: 'Heads of departments commonly kept most of the sixth-form teaching and a large part of the express stream teaching for themselves'. This was perfectly consistent with the philosophy that the real justification of a selective school was to be even more selective, and gear its curriculum to the needs of those who could achieve university entrance. The single-subject honours degree not only dictated the pattern of sixth-form specialization, and premature specialization as early as the third year of a five-year 11 to 16 course; it fostered a style of departmental organization to match. The department was no more cohesive than the school. Lacey found that although the head of department had a formal responsibility to the head for the

---

[1] C. Lacey, *Hightown Grammar* (Manchester: Manchester University Press, 1970).

teaching of his subject, 'In practice this was a relatively minor consideration, since the staff were all adequately qualified . . . and shouldered most of the responsibility themselves . . . Heads of department rarely called departmental meetings.'

All this, of course, is far removed from the assumptions and operations of a comprehensive school, and yet . . . We must remind ourselves that however noble our curriculum intentions might be, the formal structure of the typical comprehensive school curriculum bears more than a passing resemblance to that of the grammar school from which it derived. The sixth form is as specialized as ever; separate subject teaching the dominant mode; fourth- and fifth-year option schemes are an invention of the post-war grammar school, and promote a highly subject-differentiated curriculum in those years; the development of interrelated or integrated curricula is mainly confined to the first two or three years; and evidence of early specialization, of 'subject decisions . . . made as far back as the third year' was uncovered a few years ago by the Schools Council.[1]

It is, in short, still possible for the insular-minded department head to follow historical precedent, to run his own show, and leave the members of his department to run theirs. How far he is able to do this will depend on the school's approach to curriculum planning, and this will depend in turn on its response to changing influences on the curriculum. We need to consider these in order to examine the developing role of the head of department.

Recent concern for the performance of pupils at each end of the ability range is likely, in the short term, to reinforce subject demarcations. Schools are conscious of the pressure to produce more subject passes at better grades, and inevitably this is an encouragement to make the separate subject mills grind smaller still. Why bother with links between subjects, when all our energy is needed to churn out the subject results? A common assumption is that, as a corollary, formal setting into ability groups will improve pupil performance, since matching of ability to teaching material can be better organized. But, as the HMI study of gifted children in middle and comprehensive schools[2] concluded, 'Streaming is a very crude form of provision for the gifted'. The head of department must be ready to challenge conventional wisdom, even when the going is rough.

As far as the less able are concerned, a useful yardstick is

[1] *The Examination Courses of First Year Sixth Formers*, Schools Council Research Studies (Basingstoke: Macmillan Education, 1973).
[2] Department of Education and Science, *Gifted Children in Middle and Comprehensive Secondary Schools* (HMSO, 1977).

the proportion of the 16-plus age-group leaving school without a single subject grade at GCE O level or CSE. The proportion for England is now 1 in 6, compared with 1 in 4 for Wales. Neither figure gives grounds for complacency, but the poorer Welsh performance has been directly attributed to the fact that 'in spite of the overwhelming support for the comprehensive principle in most parts of Wales, the influence of the grammar school is still with us'.[1] Poor pupil engagement at the lower end of the ability range is a direct result of basing the curriculum on O-level styles of pedagogy, and diluting the mixture for less resilient stomachs. Few CSE Mode I syllabuses (or Mode III, for that matter) show evidence of radical departure from the O-level norm. And the effect of the common examination system at 16-plus may well be to retard innovation still further — at least in the short term.

There are, however, a number of influences which seek to influence or change the curriculum, and all of which limit the traditional autonomy of the head of department. They have all gathered strength during the past decade, and we can identify three in the order in which they emerged.

First, there is the argument that elements of the curriculum should be allowed to transcend their traditional subject boundaries, and exert an influence on the whole curriculum. This notion was taken up by the Bullock Report[2] on English teaching, which urged an agreed policy for each school. It was a matter not merely of English in the department, but of 'language across the curriculum'. The report recognized that this might be a matter of devising ways in which departments other than English could be made implicitly aware of what was entailed; or it might take the form of an explicit link between, say, English and history or geography in a humanities scheme. Either way (and Bullock stated no preference), the implication is clear: the English department has something to say to other departments, and other departments have an obligation to listen. In the same year, Kay[3] suggested that the work of the Assessment of Performance Unit (APU) at the Department of Education and Science should look not at subjects, but at 'lines of development': six such lines — verbal, mathematical, scientific, ethical, aesthetic, physical — were identified. The separate lines of development 'may not relate closely to subject boundaries, though subjects may well be the best way of furthering them'. The APU policy has moved

---

[1] J. Brace, 'Week by week', *Education*, (18 May 1979), p. 567.
[2] Department of Education and Science, *A Language for Life* (HMSO, 1975).
[3] B.W. Kay, 'Monitoring pupils' performance', *Trends in Education* (July 1975), pp. 11-18.

in this way, and its 1979 tests of language skills were in fact a specific recommendation of the Bullock Report.

A second influence has been political in character — the feeling that education is too important to be left simply to the professionals. Two public documents in 1977 expressed this view, if in different ways. The Taylor Report[1] on the governance of schools proposed that governing bodies should not represent a single interest group, whether public or professional. A few months later, the DES Green Paper[2] questioned the merits of fourth- and fifth-year option schemes, and declared that 'The Secretaries of State will . . . seek to establish a broad agreement . . . on a framework for the curriculum'. The autonomy of the head of department is thus further circumscribed: the curriculum he devises must be judged not merely by his own standards, or those of his team, but also by reference to other parties with a stake in the school's conduct, and by reference to the shape or framework of the whole curriculum.

A third influence derives from reasoning about the nature and purpose of compulsory education, and is justified in the HMI document *Curriculum 11–16*[3] by reference to the concepts of pupils' rights, and curriculum breadth. Asking the question, 'What have pupils a reasonable right to expect from compulsory schooling?' the document asserts that 'they have nothing less than a right' to be introduced to 'a common curriculum' that is 'broad and makes substantial claims on time'. This curriculum is defined in terms of eight 'areas of experience', which bear a close resemblance to the APU's own catechism. But it is, of course, a short logical step from the APU's evaluation of whole-curriculum effectiveness in trans-subject terms, and the Green Paper's talk of a curriculum framework, to the notion of a coherent common curriculum which makes use of subjects not so much for their own sakes, but for their contributions to forms of curriculum organization which divide up knowledge on a different basis from that of traditional subjects. These are questions which philosophers of education can help resolve, and the thinking of Hirst[4] and other educationists is evidently an influence on several of the documents that have been mentioned.

This, then, is the context in which I am going to discuss the relation between the head of department and the whole

[1] Department of Education and Science, *A New Partnership for Our Schools* (HMSO, 1977).

[2] Department of Education and Science, *Education in Schools: A Consultative Document* (HMSO, 1977).

[3] Department of Education and Science, *Curriculum 11–16* (DES, 1977).

[4] P. Hirst, 'Liberal education and the nature of knowledge', in R. Archambault (ed.), *Philosophical Analysis and Education* (Routledge & Kegan Paul, 1965).

curriculum. I am not going to take further the interplay of argument as to the meaning of 'balance' in the curriculum; the justification for a bigger core and fewer options; or the process of selecting key experiences from the culture. All these are matters of major concern not merely to department heads, but to all teachers; but they are outside my present scope. The central point is that heads of department must see themselves as front-line participants in a process of curriculum change which sees the curriculum as more than the sum of its subject parts; which recognizes that subjects interact with each other, and seeks to organize and profit from these interactions. The questions I wish to tackle are: how will the role of the department head change? what steps must he take to further both his defined subject concerns, and his responsibilities to the whole curriculum of the school?

How his role changes will depend on how the links between subjects and departments are articulated in his school. And this is a process which he must expect to be able to influence. All the evidence is that school-based change evolving within the school itself is the only effective form of curriculum change. We can usefully distinguish between a weak and a strong thesis of whole-curriculum planning. These are not intended to be pure paradigms of curriculum change; in practice, schools will probably display elements of both interpretations.

The weak thesis leads to a *policy approach*, and rests on the assumption — which may not be explicit — that putting central curriculum concerns on an inter-subject basis is primarily a matter of organization. One school, for example, has taken the APU's lines of development and appointed six co-ordinators, each responsible for one of these aspects of the curriculum. Heads of department are appointed to fourteen or so different subject responsibilities in the usual way. It is then the task of the co-ordinator for, say, science and technology to draw up a list of all the desired curriculum outcomes in this area, and establish how these are to be achieved in all the separate subjects. Or possibly a school might define its concerns differently, and determine policies — with or without co-ordinators — for important themes like moral education, or political education, or health education. The underlying organizational idea is that of a two-dimensional matrix: the subjects are along one dimension, and the unifying themes along the other. The essential connection between the two will be the ubiquitous checklist.

The strong thesis lends to a *structural approach*. The school's curriculum concerns are so defined that they can be used as the principle structuring device for the curriculum.

The underlying rationale will be made explicit by grouping subjects into curriculum areas or faculties. Thus, for example, the influence of English will be felt not through an advisory or hortatory policy document, but by virtue of its presence within a faculty grouping. Humanities might link English with history, geography and religious education; expressive arts might link it with drama and music. Equally, it could be a component of a social studies faculty, or of an aesthetic area linked with music, drama and art. The analogy with this form of organization is not the grid, as in the policy approach, but the toasting-fork. It is more strongly one-dimensional, with the faculties forming the handle of the fork, and the contributory subjects the prongs. A number of schools have come to adopt a structure of this kind, and not always for the curriculum reasons discussed here. Faculty structures are easier to timetable and offer a certain administrative tidiness.

Each approach offers some advantages, and some snags. The looser texture of the policy approach makes it more flexible: but the critical question has to be how far the policies influence classroom practice. It is one thing to get a group of teachers together and hammer out a statement of desired outcomes; it is quite another to transform these into learning experiences, even when the teachers all belong to the same subject department. Having agreed, for example, on experiences in political education that should be offered in history, geography, economics, English and religious education from the third year upwards, the co-ordinator will have his work cut out to establish that these experiences are planned, let alone effectively presented. The Scottish Munn Report[1] proposes a curriculum which retains the conventional subject structure, while aiming for a broad coverage in terms of social studies, science and the creative arts. The intention is that 'the contributions of the different subjects are so orchestrated that . . . they lead to the achievement of the established aims' — what I have termed the weak thesis. But the danger is recognized, and stated: 'The attainment of this ideal will be vitiated from the start, and the curriculum reduced to a haphazard collection of disjointed units, if subject departments, insisting on their own autonomy, simply go their separate ways.'

The strong thesis limits departmental autonomy from the start by subsuming departments within some broader curriculum grouping. The chance of translating thought into action is therefore that much greater. But the strength of that

[1] Scottish Education Department, *The Structure of the Curriculum in the Third and Fourth Years of the Scottish Secondary School* (HMSO, 1977).

approach can be its weakness; it is harder to bend or modify a faculty structure than to change a policy. To return, for instance, to the example of political education: suppose the science department adopts the Schools Council Integrated Science Project (SCISP) in the fourth and fifth years. This involves some consideration of the social influence of science, and plainly offers opportunities to extend the political competence of pupils. But it may have been agreed that these matters lie within the province of the humanities faculty. It is scarcely possible, or desirable, to move part of the science teaching to this faculty. The solution, of course, is to super-impose a policy approach[1] on the faculty structure, and hope that this will bring about the coherence you are after. It is worth adding, though, that without the structural approach to start with, the chances of the three separate subject departments coming together of their own volition and adopting an integrated or unified science programme in the fourth and fifth years must be rated as pretty slender.

How do these different views of whole-curriculum planning alter the work of the head of department? Does this new and wider emphasis make his job any easier? The answer, at first sight, is that it will add a further burden to what is a considerable load. Even if the department head in a comprehensive school has a traditionally defined role within the bounds of his subject, there are several ways in which he must do more than his grammar-school forbear. There are more teachers in the department; he operates in a context not of public approval, but of doubt; more staff and more pupils mean more administration; he will have his own teaching load; probationary teachers may be the rule, rather than the exception; he will have more to do with parents than any grammar-school teacher; and as well as all this, he will have a responsibility for the discipline within his department.

It is, then, no surprise that some recent research[2] reveals signs of stress among department heads. A survey of ninety-two comprehensive schools suggests that a major source of stress is the workload itself: 'the need to perform quite considerable administrative duties against a background of a full teaching timetable'. The two other factors generating stress turn out to be role conflict, and role confusion. Conflict arises because interaction with pupils, colleagues and parents can impose contradictory demands. Confusion arises between the roles of subject teacher, the head of a team of teachers, and perhaps tutor to student teachers as well.

[1] c.f. Appendix 2, para iv, p. 149.
[2] J. Dunham, 'Change and stress in the head of department's role',*Educational Research*, vol. 21, no. 1 (1978), pp. 44—7.

We cannot expect that in a complex activity like education, all ambiguities of role can be eliminated; and in the nature of things, we assume that a teacher promoted to departmental responsibility recognizes that more work is involved. It is a matter not only of willingness to take on extra work, but of the capacity to do it. There are important implications here for the process of selecting heads of department, which may not always be taken into account. But at the same time, it behoves us to devise ways of running schools which minimize conflict and uncertainty, and eliminate unnecessary paperwork.

This is partly a matter of good management. Many schools have given little thought to such key procedures as the ordering and distribution of stationery, for example. Some central machinery for doing this, or most of it, could lighten the load of the department head. If the initiative for this kind of reform does not come from a school's management team, then heads of departments should take the initiative and propose such arrangements. There are schools, too, where role confusion arises because no one has taken the trouble to work out guidelines for who does what. Here again, there is everything to be gained if department heads recognize the value of co-operating rather than competing with each other. By working together, they can establish a climate in which uncertainties can at least be identified, if not eliminated.

But it cannot be wholly a matter of management. Judgemental decisions are involved, because education is a value-contested area. Ordered, systematic procedures can take us so far, and make our lives a lot easier, but they cannot take us all the way. There are still central decisions to be made about the educational purpose of the school, the kinds of problems that it must seek to solve in its curriculum planning, and the kinds of ways in which these solutions are to be found. And here again I touch on issues which go beyond my present brief.

We can, however, choose strategies for whole-curriculum planning which make for clarity, and which leave as much as possible of the creative energy of department heads for thinking about the curriculum and implementing desired changes. This is why we need to be clear about the approach a school makes to a view of the whole curriculum, and the way in which it is justified. The involvement of a school's heads of departments would be essential in this process, not least because the main burden of making curriculum change work will fall on them. In particular, they will need to consider whether the policy approach gives sufficient definition and, if not, the kind of structural approach that makes the

best use of the school's resources, and best reflects its rationale
of the curriculum. They will not be alone in these considera-
tions. Developing a whole-curriculum policy must take
account of the perceptions of all staff, as well as the inclina-
tions of the head, the governors and what one might call the
school's constituency.

This is both a challenge and an opportunity. In particular,
it is an opportunity to define the head of department's role
so as to minimize the stresses which appear to afflict it at
present. I am suggesting that in linking the head of department to the whole curriculum, we are helping him, rather
than increasing his workload — providing we construct a
model for whole-curriculum planning which simplifies rather
than confuses, and promotes co-ordination rather than conflict. Take, for example, the role of the head of mathematics.
In a school operating a traditional subject-focused curriculum,
the department's parochial concern with mathematics inside
the department boundary gives it a natural inclination to
inner diversity. This first-year teacher likes the SMP work-
cards; another prefers the books; another develops his own
materials. By the fourth year, the science staff find that some
pupils have numerical skills, while others seem to lack them.
The head of department finds it difficult to put his foot
down, since mathematics-for-its-own-sake is the prevailing
policy. It is not a matter of imposing a uniform teaching
method, but rather of putting the subject in a wider educational context. If the school develops a consistent and per-
vasive policy for the mathematics curriculum, it will have set
up working parties between the various subject departments
concerned, and the head of mathematics need no longer feel
that in acknowledging, for example, the needs of the geographers for certain graphical techniques by the second year,
he is betraying the subject and likely to be thought 'soft' by
his own staff. For they, too, will have been involved in the
discussions and will be associated with the decisions. In the
same way, consider the needless confusion that can arise in
a school without a school-wide policy for pastoral matters.
Should a pupil who misbehaves in a poorly-controlled mathematics lesson be dealt with only by the teacher? Ought the
department head to intervene? Or is this a matter for the ex-
clusive attention of the year or house head? No one pretends
that there are clear-cut rules for every contingency, but it is
certain that a set of agreed guidelines to good practice can
deal with a great many cases and thus remove another area of
doubt and uncertainty.

For another example, consider the benefits there can be for
an enterprising head of geography from a school's decision to

adopt a humanities faculty as part of its structural approach to the whole curriculum. Hitherto, co-operation with the history department has been difficult, not through unreciprocated interest, but because of problems in timetabling and the allocation of space. Now it is possible to take over the top floor of the former general classroom block, or move into two adjacent huts, and blocking out the two subjects across double periods means that collaborative planning can go ahead. The proximity of the English department leads them to join in, at least for the first year; and soon the year team has worked out a unit on communications, starting with ideograms, taking in hieroglyphs, leading on to word games and anagrams and perhaps ending with a study of modern means of communication and of local transport. Related work can deal with the alphabet, theories of land use, the history of transport in the region, codes and methods of representation. All this amounts to a much richer learning environment for the whole ability range than the thin gruel often rationed out in separate subject classrooms. The contributions of the subject disciplines are distinct and unblurred, and can be taught by specialists; but the overarching theme links them together, and there seems no very good reason for organizing the programme on the basis of ability sets. The necessary resources are available for all, and by giving all pupils access to them, they can be encouraged to do their own individual best. This is not, however, to imply that individualized learning is the only way to run such a scheme; on the contrary, it will be one of a number of strategies and not necessarily the most prominent.

The fact that interrelated programmes of this kind often lead to non-streamed groups has important implications for the work of the head of department. Testing, allocating and arguing about pupils in setting schemes can take a great deal of time. The important point is that non-streaming should follow curriculum planning, as in this example, rather than precede it. Too often the latter pattern prevails, and the result, as the HMI study of mixed-ability work[1] put it, is mixed-ability grouping but not mixed-ability teaching. In theory, there is no reason why successful non-streamed teaching cannot be organized within the confines of a subject department. In practice, the prerequisite planning rarely occurs unless a school has thought about its whole curriculum. There is some logic in this: the arguments for non-streaming raise important issues about ends and means,

[1] Department of Education and Science, *Mixed Ability Work in Comprehensive Schools* (HMSO, 1978).

content and method, ideals and realities which, in their reso-
lution, determine or reflect the very ethos of a school. But
they tend only to come to the surface of the discussion when
a school is reviewing its whole curriculum strategy. By the
same token, the incentive for an individual teacher in a subject
department to question the assumptions about his work on
which he has depended for so many years will depend on his
horizons; and while these are confined by the familiar corners
of his subject, he is unlikely to become an innovator over-
night. Hence the not unfamiliar phenomenon of introducing
modern mathematics content, only to observe the same
unchanging method of traditional mathematics. This is the
drawback to piecemeal curriculum change. Once the 'pro-
jecteers' have packed their bags, there is no built-in dynamic
to take over. Most curriculum change in the 1960s and early
1970s consisted of separate subject initiatives, usually based
on an updating of subject content, and offered to schools
without any context of whole-curriculum policy. The Schools
Council, indeed, specifically eschewed any attempt to state
what a whole curriculum should look like, lest this intrude
on the autonomy of teachers in schools. Now that schools are
increasingly taking it on themselves to examine these whole-
curriculum issues, there is a much greater chance of establishing a climate of innovation in which new ideas will not only
emerge, but also take root.

Let us suppose that a new head of department has been
appointed to a school where some kind of curriculum review
is planned, or indeed under way. To what matters should he
give his prior attention? Rather than start by looking at the
strengths and shortcomings of his department, I would suggest he looks first at the links between his department and
the rest of the curriculum — and not only at what is, but also
at what might be. There are two aspects to be considered. On
the one hand, how might his subject contribute to other parts
of the curriculum? And on the other, how might other parts
of the curriculum contribute to the understanding of his
subject? Suppose a new head of science is attempting this.
Then he might notice that there is scope for links between
science and the first-year humanities work on early man. In
other years he could arrange contributions to work in music
and home economics, and in particular to work in mathematics, by offering practical applications of new techniques.
Science will contribute, too, to the health education programme organized within social studies or humanities. But
this programme will also reinforce work in human biology;
and there is a great deal mathematics can do to facilitate the
work of the science department. This sort of link is possible,

too, in work in the aesthetic and creative areas. Design problems in technology are rich sources for scientific inquiry.
And if the humanities programme incorporates, in the fourth
and fifth year, some work on philosophy, then a discussion
of the nature of the scientific method would be an admirable
starting-point.

An approach of this kind would lead our novitiate department head on a kind of grand tour, at a time when he is most
open to new ideas about the school in which he finds himself.
And it gives him a perspective against which to view the work
of his own department — indeed, a perspective on the aims
and methods of science teaching. He might, for example,
notice that while humanities teachers seem to relish a discussion of ideas, the science department runs on a diet of facts.
But how finite is a scientific fact? How far should the authority of the science teacher determine experimental outcomes?
Barnes and his collaborators[1] have described a first-year
physics lesson where pupils see whether an electric current
flows through a liquid by observing whether a bulb lights up
or a needle deflects. With one liquid, the needle moves but
the bulb stays unlit. Two pupils independently ask the
teacher why this is: 'The query was intelligent, showed evidence of curiosity and could have been used to expand the
pupils' understanding of electrical phenomena, but the teacher
said "not to worry" and to "just write down the ammeter
reading".' The teacher took a passive view of the pupils'
learning, and used his authority to discourage their involvement in the learning process. Yet this was 'in the context of
an officially "Nuffield" curriculum'.

This example illustrates not only poor science teaching in
a science lesson, but a restricted use of language which limits
the range of learning outcomes. We should not assume that
such examples are uncommon, or confined to science teaching. Rather should we conclude that there is much to be said
for greater interaction between and within departments, and
for fostering within the school an atmosphere in which self-
reflective study and discussion can flourish. We might remark,
in passing, that the example also illustrates the futility of
supposing that tests, whether local or national, can do much
to improve teaching. What matters is not the end-product,
but the learning process itself. And improving that is a task
for the school and the teachers in it, making use of the kind
of external help that can focus on operational processes and
the rationale (or lack of it) that determines them.

[1] D. Barnes, E. Sestini, B. Cooper, and I. Bliss, 'Language, power and the
curriculum', in C. Richards (ed.), *Power and the Curriculum* (Driffield: Nafferton
Books, 1978).

This is the stage, then, at which the new head of department should turn his attention to his own department, and perhaps follow this panoramic survey by producing a working paper for his department to consider. This is much better than an aimless discussion around a scratch agenda. It takes more time, but it means that arguments can be presented and developed, and either refuted or adopted. And when discussion is complete, the hope must be that what emerges is not mere compromise but some new synthesis which makes use of everyone's contributions. A vote on any issue is an admission of failure. The point about a synthesis is that something comes out of the process which was not there before; some new policy or rationale which advances understanding, rather than reinforcing the prejudice of this or that pressure group.

Ideally, an input to these discussions would be some view of the school's whole curriculum. The previous discussions between the head and other staff might, for instance, have established policies about the contribution of science to important themes such as health education; or they may have agreed that a maximum of two science subjects at 16-plus must be set, if adequate attention is to be given to other key curriculum components. Then the departmental discussions can proceed in the light of this. But if this is not the case, the outcome of the department's discussions will form a useful input, in its own right, to a wider study of the curriculum as a whole. The enterprising new head of department will lose no time in putting this outcome into the form of a revised paper, and submitting it to the head and the review body appointed to look at the whole curriculum. If no such body exists, he should point out the need for it to the head, and thus ensure that he has a seat on it.

And this, one might add, is the point at which a head should begin to reflect upon the choice of strategies open to him for whole-curriculum planning — the scope his school presents for an approach based on policies, on structural change or on some position that makes use of both. His thinking will have three elements. First, there will be some worked-out view of what an educational programme for all pupils over the years of compulsory schooling might look like. It might be based on an appraisal of HMI reports, on a process of cultural analysis, on an interpretation of the concept of a liberal education — or even on the APU's 'lines of development'. Secondly, there will be a consideration of the political context within which the curriculum must work — the choices and likely preferences of staff, parents, governors and employers. And thirdly, there must be an assessment of the talents offered by the school's staff — and, most critically, at the middle-management level of head of department, policy co-ordinator or faculty head.

It is very likely that the decision to operate a faculty structure would turn largely on whether the school's existing staff could itself produce at least some of the faculty heads — and there are many worse reasons for making this decision. Arrangements for the in-service education of heads of department are sketchy in most local education authorities, and where they do exist they tend to operate in the context of the subject rather than its relation to the rest of the curriculum. There is also an emphasis on the 'in-tray' side of departmental life; this is important, but only part of the story. In recruiting a head of faculty from outside, therefore, a head runs the risk of getting a pig in a poke. This is not to say it should not be done — that would be absurd — but that in initiating change, the fewer risks that are taken, the better. Able and imaginative heads of department should not, therefore, be reluctant to come forward. It is a difficult job, but it can be well done. And I have suggested that it is likely to be better done when it is linked with the whole curriculum than when it remains within subject confines.

It is also, without doubt, the single most important job in facilitating curriculum change. This has been noted by Waterhouse[1] who, as director of the Avon Resources for Learning Development Unit, offers a service to innovating schools:

> Staff development is not taking courses . . . [it] is a responsibility and an activity which must be thoroughly integrated with the work of the school . . . The most effective tutor for staff development is the individual's immediate superior [who] has all the advantages.

It is not enough for a head to support curriculum change: the head of department must want it to happen, and want it enough to find time to support his staff during the difficult period when the innovation is being installed and made to work. And when this is over, he must run an 'after-sales' service, stimulating discussion and underwriting new ideas with moral encouragement and the necessary resources.

Because the head of department is, as it were, the guardian of his subject and the leading interpreter in his school of the conceptual structures which give it its distinct subject shape, he has a responsibility to use this authority as generously as possible. Rather than retreat behind his subject wall into a well-sandbagged position, and repel the advances of those bearing other banners, he should make it his business to seek

[1] P. Waterhouse, 'Staff development in two contexts', in C. Richards (ed.), *New Contexts for Teaching, Learning and Curriculum Studies* (Bolton: Association for the Study of the Curriculum, 1977).

out new ways of using his subject's expertise. Consider, for example, the problem of one-year sixth-form courses. There are very few school sixth forms where the provision for these courses is reckoned to be entirely satisfactory, and it ranks high on any list of sixth-form problems. Some help might have come from the Certificate of Extended Education (CEE), but it will not be continued. A number of schools have made use of City and Guilds foundation courses, which operate on a quite different basis. Instead of pupils making up a programme from single-subject GCE O-level or CEE choices, a foundation course fills the whole timetable (or most of it), and makes use of subjects to illuminate the course theme, which serves as a focus of interest for the whole course. Whether a course has engineering or community care as its vocational theme, it will contain the six core elements of industrial and environmental studies; skills and practices; technology, theory and science; communication studies; guidance education; and optional activities such as music, hobbies, etc. The course poses to teachers the question: how does the subject matter I am teaching contribute to the total desired outcomes of the curriculum? Schools Council Working Paper 45[1] argued that 'teachers have been brought up in their subjects and they think in subject terms'. But this is to miss the point, which is to make use of subjects as part of a co-herent course. The fact that every year more schools take up City and Guilds foundation courses suggests that teachers are prepared to make the necessary adjustment, for the sake of what they must regard as a worthwhile piece of curricular innovation. Their views of their subject specialisms, in short, are not immutably linked to the single-subject examination; teachers are recognizing that subjects have much to offer each other.

But in all initiatives of this kind, the attitudes of the head of department can be decisive. We need to foster in department heads the principle that a readiness to use subject skills as a window on the rest of the curriculum, rather than the bars of a prison, is the mark of strength as opposed to weakness. There is also, of course, the wider aspect of a teacher's professionalism: there is much to be said for encouraging teachers to see themselves as educators rather than subject specialists. A doctor may have a specialist knowledge of gynaecology, but we still expect him to treat us for earache. His specialist knowledge advances, rather than limits, his professionalism. Teachers, on the other hand, have allowed

---

[1] *16–19: Growth and Response*, 1. Curricular Bases (Evans/Methuen Educational, 1972).

themselves to be thought of as plumbers; just as you would not expect a plumber to re-plaster the ceiling, so you would not expect a teacher of mathematics to argue the case for or against integrated science. But why ever not? Whatever a teacher's subject, he needs to reflect on its place in the curriculum, and hence on those underlying educational issues which must inform his judgement.

The head of department, then, has everything to gain — both for himself and for his team of teachers — from seeing his role in terms of the curriculum of the whole school. His job must be to provide a perspective for understanding how his department selects and implements learning experiences, and to establish a tradition of critical, reflexive thinking. The basis of this will be examples of practice, which can serve as the means by which actions can be justified and the criteria for judging them elaborated and refined. By reflecting on the work of pupils, and the curriculum decisions that underlie pupil activities, he can build up a pattern of deliberation — a recognition that curriculum problems are uncertain, involve an adjudication between competing goals and values, and that there are no right answers, only defensible ones. Such a process must lead inexorably to a consideration of whole-curriculum concerns, and this can only enrich the work of the department and of the entire school.

2 The head of department and the school

George Phipson

A newly appointed head of department will naturally be most concerned with issues within his department and it may be some time before he begins to examine the role of his department, and he as its head, in the context of the rest of the school. But the relationship of the department to the rest of the school is vital to both, and it is towards developing such fruitful and constructive relationships that we now turn.

The new head of department must begin to understand the organization and structure of the school, perhaps starting with some introduction to this on an induction day or course or by consulting a staff guide. But even then it may still not be clear exactly who is responsible for what. Certainly a check-list would include:

1 Establishing the lines of delegated responsibilities
2 The broad structure — academic, pastoral, etc.
3 The elements of the curriculum — compulsory, options, sixth form, etc.
4 The methods of pupil grouping — mixed ability, house-based, vertical tutor groups, etc.
5 Who meets with whom, how often, and what then happens
6 The hidden structures and values (the note or the chat, or both).

Much of this is frequently encapsulated in an organizational diagram such as in Figure 2.1. This diagram may well be an over-simplification of a real school situation — and one can have a great deal of sympathy for the deputy services! But it will serve to make the point that such diagrams essentially show the lines of communication *from the head* and are in a sense no more than an *aide-mémoire* for the head of the way he delegates his responsibilities.

Our head of department needs in effect to redraw the diagram from his point of view — as in Figure 2.2. Now each radiating line is a contact that must be made; a relationship

Figure 2.1   School organization

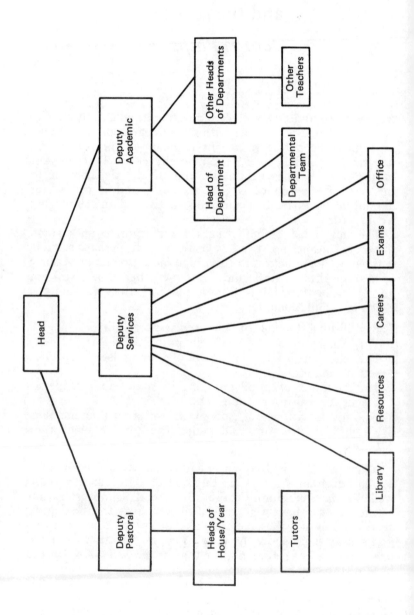

Figure 2.2   School organization from the viewpoint of the head of department

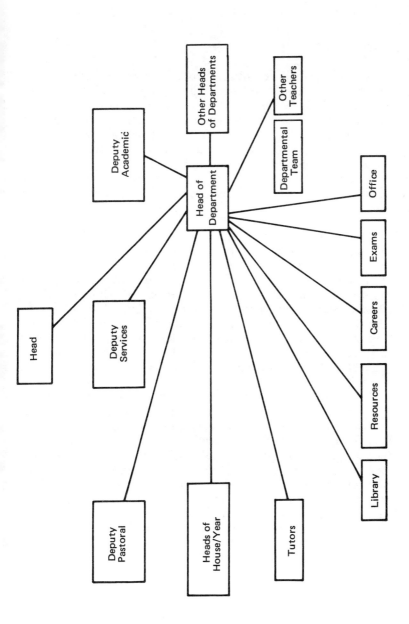

which must be developed. Our task here is to examine some
of the issues involved in establishing these relationships by
looking in turn at the key areas indicated or implied in the
second diagram.

The head

Since the head is responsible for all aspects of the school,
there is a natural tendency within any school to wish to
consult him if in doubt. Thus relations with the head must
necessarily be one of balancing his unique position and
ultimate responsibility for the whole school with his in-
ability to have the time to deal with every matter, and thus
his need to delegate.

A number of guiding principles seem to emerge from
this. First, a head will be anxious to be kept well informed;
therefore pass on news of developments – of good things
as well as worries. Then, when the need to consult does
arise, the head is well briefed. Going to a head late on a
matter he has heard nothing about previously will not en-
dear a head of department to him. At the same time, if
a head has carefully set up a structure of delegated responsibility and then meets instances of short-circuiting
this, it seems legitimate for him to redirect the matter to
the appropriate point in the structure. Indeed, if these
instances come from a head of department, then it must
beg the question of how well the delegated structure is
understood by someone who holds responsibilities derived
from it.

One distinct area in which the relationship between
head and head of department needs special consideration
is over the matter of staff and their careers. Leaving aside
the important issues involved in staff appointment and
concentrating on staff already appointed, it is clear that
the good head of department will always be sensitive to
the professional development and progress of the departmental staff. However, references and testimonials will
normally be requested from the head, and the staff themselves will naturally, on occasions, want to consult the
head in confidence. At the other, unhappy, extreme, where
the work of a member of staff does not seem to reach even
minimum standards, it will ultimately rest with the head
to pursue the matter. So perhaps the aim of keeping the
head fully informed becomes even more important when
it concerns the professional development of staff.

Consultative process

As part of a structure of delegation of responsibilities it is reasonable to expect to find within a school some form of consultative process. At the very least some sort of meeting of senior staff will take place and regular heads of department meetings seem a reasonable expectation. The role of an individual head of department attending such a meeting has been likened to that of a Cabinet Minister attending Cabinet,[1] and certainly has three distinct aspects: representing the interests of his department, acting as a specialist adviser and implementing agreed policies.

The first of these, representing the interests of his department, will involve, at various times, fighting, explaining, compromising and conceding. Almost all heads of department can clearly see their role here and may indeed be only too keen to forward the interests of their subject. At last they have the opportunity to see their area properly represented and its needs and difficulties recognized. However, it is sadly obvious at such meetings that many of those present see their role as extending no further than fighting for their own subject.

The second aspect, that of specialist adviser, is less dramatic and requires much unseen hard work, but when a school policy is being formulated it is both in the interests of the head of department's subject area and in the wider interests of the school that his view as a specialist should be heard. This may well mean attending after-school meetings of the Curriculum Standing Committee or a specially convened working party; or it may mean not leaving unread yet another discussion document. If new arrangements for, say, grades or second-language extraction, prove unsatisfactory to his area, his advice may well by then be too late. Undoubtedly the greater the breadth of view of a head of department, the more weight his views will carry.

The third aspect, interpreting school policy back in the department, may on occasions prove the most taxing. If the policy is in line with his own views, then the task should be easy. The challenge comes in showing the same strength of leadership in implementing a policy about which he has doubts. It is his job to see that the policy is carried out, and it will be to him that lapses in his department and among his staff will be referred. A frequent cry from the heart of teachers is that things would be much easier if only the school

---

[1] Michael Marland, *Head of Department* (Heinemann Educational Books, 1971), p. 90.

could agree on some common standards. Once agreed, the head of department has a clear part to play in seeing that they are adopted.

The overall success of a consultative process must depend on the ability of those consulted to be well prepared, having had time to gather views and consider implications. Hence a consultative process is virtually as good as its agendas. Much can be said of the need to bring forward proposals in good time, with adequate supporting documents and clear indications of the point to be agreed and the expected actions that will follow. Drawing up an agenda will encompass all this, and incidentally puts substantial power in the hands of the person doing it!

Democratic process

The previous section examined the role of head of department as an attender of meetings; here, briefly, it is appropriate to consider him as a convener of meetings. The head of department who has consulted his own department on the agenda for the next heads of department meeting can speak with far greater confidence, yet the teaching profession seems on occasions to find difficulty in deciding when the consultative process becomes a democratic process. There are, for example, schools which bring before a whole staff meeting the proposed allocations of money for the coming year, while in other schools this is a well-guarded secret of the head. A head of department who thinks back to the time before he took on such onerous responsibilities may well recall the frustration of not feeling that his views were heard. Indeed this may well have been the spur to seeking promotion.

In greatly over-simplifying the whole subject, it is nonetheless worthwhile considering what can be deduced as to the role and function of meetings in schools by looking at their size and frequency. A classic arrangement is: whole staff, once a term; heads of department, once a month; heads of house or year, once a week. How often then should a department meet?

Academic organization

While it would be comforting to be able to assume that those meetings held as part of a consultative process included representatives from all parts of the school organization, it is worth looking in greater detail at the specific issues likely, for example, to be part of the overall responsibility of an academic deputy or director of studies. In particular, one could hope to find someone with oversight of the balance of the curriculum and the distribution of resources.

The able head of science who has successfully drawn resources away from, say, mathematics should not then complain about the problem of poor mathematics among his science students. Less obviously, but just as importantly, a full afternoon of creative arts in the lower school may force upper-school options (which include art) into the morning, thus leaving upper school English and mathematics predominantly in the afternoon. The ability of any individual to investigate such situations and try to quantify the effects will depend on the amount of information which is made available. But even given only a school timetable, a pretty thorough curriculum analysis can be undertaken so that it should be possible to establish where the curriculum 'bonus' is being deployed.[1] In a school where information about the allocation of money is also available, further analysis can be made. As an example, Figure 2.3 looks at the three areas forming one faculty in 1978/79 in an Inner London Education Authority school where the 'marginal' cost of an extra teacher is a realistic consideration.

Figure 2.3   Analysis of departmental resources

1 Staff
(a) Cost of an extra teacher under the Inner London Education Authority AUR (Alternative Use of Resources) scheme for 1978/79 was £5145
(b) £5145 ÷ 40 weeks ÷ 35-period week gives cost of a teacher-period as £3.68
(c) Staff cost per period per pupil depends on group size:

MATHS	SCIENCE	HOME ECONOMICS
30 pupils = 12p each	20 pupils = 18p each	15 pupils = 24p each

2 Capitation
This was distributed on a pupil-period x weighting and gave:

MATHS	SCIENCE	HOME ECONOMICS
1p per pupil period	2½p per pupil-period	7p per pupil-period

3 Total resources per pupil per period

MATHS	SCIENCE	HOME ECONOMICS
12p + 1p = 13p	18p + 2½p = 20½p	24p + 7p = 31p

4 Example of other resources — rooms

MATHS	SCIENCE	HOME ECONOMICS
7 rooms for 10 staff	8 rooms for 9 staff	3 rooms for 3 staff

[1] See T. I. Davis, *School Organization* (Oxford: Pergamon, 1969); also *Curriculum Analysis and Planning* (Inner London Education Authority, 1977).

There is a great danger of such analyses and comparisons being used solely to support and further the claims of one area; but a more constructive attitude is to try to achieve a fair balance of resources across the whole curriculum. Indeed it would seem fair to picture some form of accountability, so that the department which is receiving a generous allowance of resources is both able to show the way in which they have been used to good effect, and is also aware of what other departments have been able to achieve while making do with less. Just as education in general has to argue its case for scarce national resources, so, too, within a school the deployment of scarce resources must be well thought out.

Academic partners

Besides considering the place of a department in the full academic organization, it is necessary to develop special relations with related departments. Most heads of department will certainly want to develop close links with the remedial department, for example. Their subject may also be a part of some integrated course. A head of history, for example, may be working under a head of mankind in the lower school, while having independent courses in the upper school. Indeed the arguments for and against such integrated courses having a separate leader, or being run jointly by the contributing areas, are instructive, and certainly the relationships will be very different under the two alternative arrangements.

Even where no integrated course exists, many areas have natural partners such as mathematics and science, or biology and health. In some school organizations these groupings can form the basis of faculty groups. Certainly, where a faculty structure is nothing more than a grouping together of departments under departmental heads, then, as Cyril Poster[1] has pointed out, little has been achieved in the new organization. There can be no final answer, but while faculties probably aid co-operation and communication within each faculty, they may well create larger divides to be bridged between each faculty. For a head of department no structure will replace the essential but often time-consuming task of developing close and regular contacts with these related areas.

[1] Cyril Poster, *School Decision-making* (Heinemann Educational Books, 1976), p. 33.

Pastoral structure

Relations between academic heads and pastoral heads often seem to be fraught with tension, which can sadly prevent constructive and fruitful understanding. The key seems to be to understand the essential difference of role: pastoral responsibility is for the whole school experience of those pupils in the house or year; academic responsibility is for the experience of all pupils in that one area. Thus the difficulties of a pupil in one area being dealt with by the head of that area can only be related to other difficulties and problems via the pastoral team; each needs to and must work closely with the other.

However, even within a smoothly working arrangement, problems can occur which seem to stem from a confusion of status and function. A tutor's function may involve him in raising a matter with a head of department whose status may seem impressive, yet few headteachers would use their status to discipline a pupil without consulting the person whose function it is to know the pupil pastorally. The well-known maxim that every effective classroom teacher is also concerned pastorally is now further borne out by the fact that most teachers are also tutors.

Unfortunately, the pastoral/academic divide is frequently built in to the structure with, for example, a deputy head in charge of each. (My own sub-headings here have separated the two for convenience.) Indeed what seem to be sensible administrative arrangements can only further enlarge the divide. Does, for example, the main consultative meeting of the school involve both heads of department and of house/year? Do the pupil teaching groups relate to houses and do staff teach predominantly pupils from specific houses? There are so many aspects of school organization which need maximum co-operation, that close and constructive relations must be forged — for example, in option choices and their career implications, referral to sanctuary/support unit, and requests for changes of groups. The list is endless because in effect it covers every vital part of school life. It is only to be regretted that the demands of running large departments sometimes result in heads of major departments giving up tutoring. Regretted because not only have such experienced staff a great deal to offer as tutors, but also as part of a pastoral team they are helping to break down any lack of mutual understanding.

Whole-school issues

Certainly since the publication of the Bullock Report[1] schools have come to recognize that some issues require a concerted approach across the whole school. A new head of department needs to review the department's place in, and contribution to, such policies. Besides a policy for language across the curriculum,[2] schools may well have formulated policies for numeracy, careers, and so on.

Other matters dealt with across the school as a whole may well include an induction programme for new staff under a teacher-tutor, in-service training in general and the placement of student-teachers. Here the head of department must be aware of what is being done centrally and what is left to individual departments.

It is also appropriate to remember that besides the formally arranged whole-school issues, many such matters are raised and discussed and decisions made over cups of coffee at break. Thus the successful department with a comfortable and well-appointed headquarters room may be in danger of being isolated from some of the vital issues of the school.

Services

Besides the actual teaching staff, every school has a small army of staff keeping the school running. Without exception these people can be of immense value and help to the teaching staff, and the rule for a head of department seems to be to make contact and establish relations before he actually finds himself seeking such help. Some key areas are:

The library. This should not be thought of as the province of English alone. A new syllabus may well require some fresh titles in the library. In fact establishing what books in the department's area are being taken out is very useful feedback.

The resources centre. What is available and how is it booked? What specialist help and advice can be tapped? Often the challenge is to balance central resources with departmental resources.

The school office. The pressures on the school office are frequently underrated by teachers and there may well be

---

[1] Department of Education and Science, *A Language for Life* (HMSO, 1975).
[2] See Recommendation 139 of the Bullock Report; also Michael Marland, et al., *Language Across the Curriculum: The Implementation of the Bullock Report in the Secondary School* (Heinemann Educational Books, 1977).

a case for a school having separate facilities for typing and duplicating of teaching material.

The caretaker. He probably knows the true state of class-room discipline better than even the head, and knows it on a department by department basis!

Kitchen staff, dinner ladies, medical room attendant, etc., all play a vital part and want to be as useful as possible so that, for example, problems over medical inspections which cut across practical sessions in the department can easily be resolved with a friendly word.

Outside the school

A head of department needs to give some time and thought to people not actually working in the school but who are equally important in the total picture. Advisory teachers, inspectors and teachers' centre staff spring readily to mind. Even the more anonymous officers at County Hall may prove useful allies when a special project is in the air. It is perhaps a sad reflection that we can see the school governing body, the local primary school, and even the parents, as 'outsiders'. Frequently such people are only waiting for an invitation to be involved, and a head of department who arranges, say, an open evening to show them the work of the department may be doing an enormous amount to break down barriers. In fact governors and parents are very often keen to be asked to contribute in some way and will be only too happy to do what they can to help if a head of department explains the need — for example, for a piece of equipment, or for a local firm to be visited as part of a course.

Keeping relations sweet

The paragon of virtue and ability who has successfully estab-lished relations with the rest of the school as indicated should perhaps give a moment's thought to keeping them that way. Day-to-day experience in school shows that the single greatest irritant is covering lessons for absent colleagues, so the first rule is not to need cover! But there is no doubt that the departments that provide a list of pupils plus suitable work for a covering teacher are valued. Comparisons between departments are also going to be made by those staff who teach in more than one area and again the well-organized department will more easily attract staff who will then spread the word round the school. Another potential source of irritation can be badly planned trips and outings that disrupt the teaching of other subjects because proper arrangements have not been made in advance.

In a more positive sense, a good head of department is going to look for ways to contribute to the life of the school and at the same time provide a good public image for the department. Some of these ways are obvious — the English department publishing a magazine, the music department organizing concerts. Any department will benefit from working together at anything, from a stall at the summer fair to a turn in the Christmas comedy show.

Conclusions

The head of department venturing outside his department to establish relations with the rest of the school will be a more or less effective 'foreign secretary' depending on two issues — the extent to which this is seen as part of the responsibilities of the role, and the extent to which the school is organized to encourage such relationships.

In the sections above there have been some guiding themes. Openness — the open school encourages much of what has been advocated; in a school which seems closed then perhaps the moment is right to start to reverse the trend. Constructiveness — only seeing the role as fighting for your own area will mean opportunities missed; if all the contributory parts are looking to the common good, all will benefit. Accountability — the resources a department obtains and how it uses them is the concern of the whole school, and within the school must be reviewed as thoroughly as the schools themselves are under scrutiny for nationally scarce resources. Defensiveness — this is perhaps a natural reaction to a close examination by others, but we must resist the temptation to want to 'be left to run my own department on my own'. Perspective — the wider the perspectives of a head of department, the more valuable his contribution to the school as a whole. Showmanship! — a good head of department is in part doing a PR job for the department, and staff are happier teaching in a department which is seen as successful.

While having great sympathy with the cry that the internal responsibilities of a department are time-consuming enough, a strong plea is made for due consideration of a department's role within the school. The head of department who manages both will have improved mutual understanding and respect and made the school a richer institution for its pupils.

3 The qualities of a good head of department

Colin Bayne-Jardine

Surprisingly little has been written about the task of the head of department in a secondary school in England and Wales. There can be no question that the post of head of department is prized and Michael Marland[1] has pointed out that many foreign observers regard the post as the 'driving force behind curriculum revision in the school'. The powers and indeed the tasks are not laid down nationally, and in some schools they are ill-defined and hardly ever discussed. In a research project written up by Geoffrey Lyons[2] for Bristol University, the dual responsibility of virtually all heads of department is highlighted, as they are expected to act as a tutor or form teacher to a pupil group though their principal commitment within the school is to teaching. The task is complex and the demands made upon heads of department are importunate. There is no simple way in which a check-list of good qualities or a long list of tasks could be produced. However, John Adair[3] has written: 'So far research has not thrown up any gold rules that can legitimately be transferred to the world of the manager, but it has enlarged our understanding and stimulated our imagination'. This chapter is an attempt to enlarge the understanding of, and to stimulate imagination about, the head of department's job, and then to suggest some qualities demanded for a good performance. Above all it is vital to remember that the task is not static and not repetitive. Human beings are at its heart, and the head of department has to be a sensitive communicator and purposeful controller. The description of Mother in the kitchen in Laurie Lee's *Cider With Rosie*[4] catches this element. The children are gathered as evening draws in. All are involved in a variety of activities from slashing away at

---

[1] Michael Marland, *Head of Department* (Heinemann Educational Books, 1971).
[2] G. Lyons, *The Administrative Tasks of Head and Senior Teachers in Large Secondary Schools* (Bristol: University of Bristol, 1974), pp. 77–85.
[3] J. Adair, *Training for Decisions* (Farnborough: Gower Press, 1978), p. 89.
[4] Laurie Lee, *Cider With Rosie* (Harmondsworth: Penguin Books, 1962), p. 72.

'William Tell' on the violin to doing 'inscrutable homework'. When gathered for tea they grabbed, dodged, passed and snatched, and packed their mouths like pelicans. 'Mother ate always standing up, tearing crusts off the loaf with her fingers, a hand-to-mouth feeding that expressed her vigilance, like that of a wireless-operator at sea'.

With this crucial point in mind the head of department's job can be set in a broad perspective. First, the historical background is important. In the period immediately after 1944 heads and administrators who had thrived in the strictly hierarchical environment of the armed forces wished to see their new commands divided into clearly defined cohorts with themselves at the top and with heads of department corresponding to the company commander.[1] Such a system fits uneasily into an age which demands flexibility. In fact it is possible to analyse the ways which heads of department have used to match their historical role with changes in both organization of schools and of subject matter. A number of 'pathologies' have been described by Eric Hoyle[2] and these do give an interesting insight into the way that the working of a subject department and curriculum development can be rendered difficult by the unquestioning acceptance of an ill-defined and inappropriate role. The 'ritualist' head of department hides behind detail: tidy mark lists, registers of textbooks, colour codes, and departmental discussion about the examination board to be used rather than about the examinations. The 'neurotic' worries ineffectually about the problems of carrying theory into practice. Lengthy study of publishers' lists can end with a late book order and a department's plans in ruins. The bright young head of department often resorts to the 'robber baron' pattern. He drives his department on to give the impression of effectiveness. Often the members of the department are left to pick up the pieces after the innovating head of department has left for promotion. Aspects of such pathologies will appear in many cases but they can become a dominant response under pressure, and too often the most respected and effective teacher opts out of the organization and becomes the 'rebel' by withdrawing into the classroom.

Secondly, the head of department must be seen as doing a job with a real sense of purpose within a school organization as a whole. This sense of purpose can best be derived when a school harnesses the talents of its staff effectively. The

[1] C. Bayne-Jardine and C. Hannam, 'Heads of departments?', *Forum*, vol. 15, no. 1 (1972), pp. 29–30.
[2] E. Hoyle, *The Role of the Teacher* (Routledge & Kegan Paul, 1969), pp. 51–3.

climate should encourage rational curriculum planning along the lines outlined by Malcolm Skilbeck[1] among others. A situational analysis in a subject area will be followed by careful planning, preparation, implementation in the classroom, and evaluation. Such a systematic approach must infuse all levels of a school if it is to have a sense of purpose.

Finally, in this broad perspective it is vital to remember that the job should contain pleasure. The subject department in a secondary school will only really be alive if its members remember that study can provide pleasure and enrichment. It will be a sad and gloomy time when there is no acceptance of the enjoyment to be gained from study. Goldsmith's village schoolmaster should be remembered:

> If severe in aught
> The love he bore to learning was in fault

From this general setting the focus upon the area in which the head of department will display qualities can be narrowed. Jack Dunham[2] has suggested a number of functions that ought to be considered as the main ones for heads of department:

1 Communication with the head or other senior staff to win resources or status for the department. At one level such communication may seek to gain a proper understanding of a subject and its needs.
2 Communication with other departments and with the pastoral organization. This may well be complicated by the fact that the pastoral organization may not match the teaching groups at all, particularly when an option scheme is introduced in the fourth year.
3 Communication with members of the department either as individuals or in groups. This is the crucial area in which the head of department has to use the appropriate leadership skills to motivate, to reduce anxiety and frustration, and to develop the sense of purpose and effectiveness already mentioned.
4 Communication with parents about the pupils and teachers.
5 Administration, including planning, organizing and budgeting.
6 Teaching.
7 Staff selection and staff development.

These then are seven areas in which a head of department

---

[1] M. Skilbeck, 'School based curriculum development', in J. Walton and J. Welton (eds), *Rational Curriculum Planning* (Ward Lock Educational, 1976).
[2] J. Dunham, 'Change and stress in the head of department's role', *Educational Research*, vol. 21, no. 1 (1978), pp. 44–7.

has to work. I will now suggest five qualities which might make for a good head of department.

The ability to co-operate and communicate must be first of the five qualities. A head of department cannot be effective if he is unable to relate to the school as a whole. With the complex curriculum designs in secondary schools all subjects must interlock, and those responsible should be prepared to discuss matters such as language across the curriculum. Sometimes a head of department may feel that the school organization is too closed and that his subject can only thrive by going to war with others. This sort of market-place competition can only be destructive and so there is a vital need for the ability to communicate. A good head of department will be able to work with senior staff to create a co-operative climate. Very few people will turn away from a genuine offer of co-operation and help. The sort of area that can be opened for discussion is the allocation of capitation and the priorities of the school.

The ability to observe and to listen is the second quality. Too often people become prisoners of the expectations of others or of their own expectations. At a heads of department meeting some members may well take a set position and fail to observe or listen. Such set positions mean frustration and an end to learning and development.

Thirdly, the good head of department should be able to manage resources efficiently and without fuss. Routine administrative tasks are a matter of good organization and management. It should never be a point of pride that book orders, class lists, examination entries, reports, are in a muddle and often late because in some way they are beneath proper consideration. A head of department will only get the best out of the members of the department if the basic administration is well ordered and efficient.

Fourthly, the quality of forward planning. The head of department will need to keep in touch with the major developments in a subject area as well as with ideas about curriculum planning and design. In the Munn Report[1] the point is made that any curriculum would be a defective one if it exalted one set of claims, stemming from social, epistemological and psychological approaches, above others. This reconciliation of competing claims at different levels of a school is vitally important for a head of department.

Finally, the good head of department should be able to delegate within the department. The effective department

[1] Scottish Education Department, *The Structure of the Curriculum in the Third and Fourth Years of the Scottish Secondary School* (HMSO, 1977).

within a school will be a loosely-linked group of individuals with the co-ordinating department head. He must have the patience to work within the complex context of the secondary school. He must have the intellectual clarity to conceptualize the methods of working as a group and the persuasiveness to mobilize the members of the department team so that they know and understand the goals to be worked towards and are prepared to share the task. Good leaders have always been generalists yet it is sometimes difficult for a subject specialist to take up a position from which they have a view of a broader horizon. It is only with this sort of broad perspective and a readiness to trust others and delegate that the head of department will be able to cope with the multiple demands of modern school organizations. The good head of department will know his own strengths and weaknesses and be aware of the strengths and weaknesses of the members of his team. A sensible and systematic approach to in-service staff development will be one feature of such a department.

The typical description of the head of department's job in a secondary school might read as follows:

> The person appointed will be expected to work with colleagues in designing and implementing the curriculum throughout the school. He or she is responsible to the head for the teaching of the subject throughout the school. He or she will be expected to advise on developments in subject teaching and examining, on staffing and timetable details. He or she will provide and revise schemes of work and reading schemes, and will maintain records of departmental meetings. Co-ordination of policy within the department and leadership of subject staff, including guidance to probationer teachers, are vital elements of the job. Oversight of subject teaching, methods and standards of work throughout the school, as well as requisition and control of stationery, stock and equipment, will also be expected.

Such a task demands all the qualities outlined in this chapter and the vital human touch. J. G. Owen[1] outlines the qualities of the person who will fit well into a creative organization and suggests that anyone fitting his composite definition would be a paragon. Nevertheless the qualities demanded centre on ideas such as openness, risk-taking, freedom from too much outside pressure, and freedom from hierarchical rigidities. The military metaphor used to describe the origins of the head of department earlier points up the need to ensure the development of a new set of attitudes and assumptions towards the role. The good head of department must know himself, understand a complex task and be able to work in and to foster an open climate within a school.

[1] J. G. Owen, *The Management of Curriculum Development* (Cambridge: Cambridge University Press, 1973), pp. 92–3.

PART TWO

Assessment, Evaluation and Development

Chapters 4, 5 and 6 look in depth at three areas of responsibility crucial to effective department leadership. They are, however, among the least thought about and most poorly dealt with. The practicality of these chapters should assist and encourage those of us who tend to delay consideration of such difficult issues owing to the pressure of seemingly more urgent priorities. A clear understanding of the problems, needs and performance of teachers and pupils is obviously essential to good management.

4 Professional development of teachers within the department

Michael Marland

There are many nice sounding phrases in education which no-body can be against; these are the stock phrases for platforms and journalistic articles, groups of words which sound as if they must indicate 'a good thing' and which rarely have their meaning challenged. However, what we should do to implement such phrases is rarely worked out in detail. Such a phrase is 'professional development', or its related variant: 'career development'. The purpose of this chapter is to make these vague, high-sounding ambitions more tangible, to break them down and analyse them so that we can see how we actually set about doing something about the idea as a head of department.

We all come into teaching interested in our subjects and working with children. Teachers are good at taking responsibility for children. However, when we take a responsibility post in a school, we are taking responsibility for other adults. I wonder whether we face quite clearly enough the pain and the tension that such a responsibility involves. Indeed, as teachers are we always temperamentally suitable to take responsibility for other adults? Certainly, we have to adjust quite considerably to be able to do it. Of all those responsibilities for adults which we undertake, that for their development as professionals is arguably the most important and the most difficult. Yet the moment a teacher becomes a head of department he has entered into the in-service training business. In fact one way of looking at a department is to see it primarily as an in-service training enterprise. The importance of this part of the job is clear when we realize that without it all the other responsibilities that a head of department has for the curriculum and the care of pupils will not flourish. It is a responsibility logically prior to all the other responsibilities.

Comparisons suggest that this is a task we do not carry out very well. Although we often consider schools to be primarily concerned with personal relations and human growth, and industry to be primarily concerned with productivity, many industrial and commercial firms are much better at the career and professional development of their staff than we are in schools. It is almost as if a good commercial firm really values the growth of its staff, but the education service takes it for granted. I learned this most fully during the years when I was head of Woodberry Down School and it was 'twinned' with IBM's city office. In that firm the responsibility of the line managers for the development of their staff is clearly spelled out, and there are a series of related courses to assist them. Even the plight of the person who comes into the firm with a somewhat limited general education is considered in terms of his future personal needs: for instance, junior management are offered a six-week course on a wide variety of aspects of modern life. This course is not immediately job-related, but foresees the individual's needs for later, wider growth. In comparison with that firm's total programme for planned career development, a local education authority's programme for in-service education looks frankly fragmented, amateur and sparse.

I have also noticed that the quality of a team in a department reveals quite clearly how the head of department perceives this aspect of his role. It is very interesting when you interview candidates for a head of department post. Maybe there are five short-listed candidates who have come for a job as head of department. As the evening goes on, you realize from the candidates' answers, and even their questions, that you are really interviewing the distant head of department of the candidate. He is not present, but his influence is. Time and time again the candidates reveal by their attitudes or their knowledge not only their own personal qualities, but also the kind of leadership they have been given by their head of department. Sometimes it is impossible to see individuals as a potential head of department because they have worked in a team with such a poor head of department that they do not really know what the title means. This is, of course, a very serious indictment of their own head of department, whose career development plans have been so poor.

Of course, I appreciate that we are all individuals and must also help ourselves. I am not suggesting that the head of department plays a superperson role and actually arranges all the personal growth and development of the staff. I am suggesting, however, that the head of department must facilitate this growth. The task is made difficult by two factors. The first is well described by David Hargreaves, an educational sociologist, in a study called 'What teaching does to teachers'.[1] The job brings its own special emotional exhaustion which

---

[1] David Hargreaves, 'What teaching does to teachers', *New Society*, vol. xx, 1979.

Hargreaves declares, can produce apathy. He claims that one effect of the job is that teachers become bad learners; they stop listening and exploring, and so are difficult to teach. Although he is probably over-stating his case, he describes a problem that we have to recognize. In looking towards ways of helping our staff develop, we have to admit that perhaps we are sometimes so busy giving out that we are not so good at taking in.

The second factor is that there is a series of tensions in the needs of career development of teachers. These can be laid out in a series of antitheses:

formal	informal
planned	spontaneous
team needs	individual needs
task-focused	person-focused

These are too often seen as mutually exlusive — either/or options. In fact the problem is not in choosing one or the other, but in obtaining an appropriate balance between the two.

Taking the first pair: if you never have an informal chat, there will not be much of a team; but if you do not set up semi-formal events as well, important aspects will be missed out in the work with teachers. Similarly, with the second pair: of course, a head of department must be sensitive enough to rise to the moment — for instance, to pick up the chance remark that someone makes. 'It would be good to teach craft', an art teacher might say casually over coffee. This is the kind of passing remark that a head of department has to grab onto and follow up. Equally, though, a head of department has to *anticipate* and to plan.

The next tension is between team needs and individual needs. Each teacher in the team has individual strengths and weaknesses, and individual needs. If professional development is left entirely to self-expressed individual needs, people build only on their strengths. At first that sounds fine, but actually the other side of that is that those people don't grow much in their areas of weakness. If a head of department leaves things too much to individual needs, he will find that all the applications for in-service work, everything that is read, and all the courses attended, merely reinforce the aspects the teachers are already rather good at. That may be useful if as head of department you want them to be the main experts in your team in that particular field. However, it may be the one thing they need to do is actually to concentrate on those things at which they are weak. Thus a head of department also needs to look at team needs to make sure

that the overall balance is right in the team. You may therefore need to persuade somebody to become more expert in
something about which they know little so far; it may not be
necessary for their individual development, but it may be
necessary for your team's development.

The last tension is between what I call task-focused and
individual-focused work. By task-focused development I
mean that the departmental team has a task. It may be
realized, for instance, that a department is not very good at
the teaching of non-narrative reading, and yet they have got
to do it because the pupils must learn from reading books.
Therefore, we may seek or create some method of developing these skills. However, as individuals, people also have
more personal, even more idiosyncratic needs, and these must
not be left out. If a teacher wants to have time off or support
to go on a particular course that seems to be startlingly
irrelevant, it may still be very important to him as an individual, and you may need to take that into consideration and
support the request. This last point is doubly important in
times of stability. Then it may be extra important to help
people with personal interests that they would have liked to
follow up before if they had had a chance.

The task that faces the head of department in facilitating
the professional development of his teachers divides into five
sections: initial training with students; induction work with
new teachers, be they probationers or not[1]; responsibilities
and planning within a department, which I want to describe
from the point of view of the development of professional
skills; in-service work; and career development.

Initial training

Every school needs to have an overall plan for students. Not
all schools do, however, and if your school does not, it is
vital that as a head of department you work towards getting
such a plan going. You may be in a school with a professional
tutor of one sort or another, or a senior teacher in charge of
students, who is responsible for an overall school policy. If
you are not, you should get on the heads of departments'
agenda your suggestion that the school needs such an overall
policy. If you are in the sort of school where you consider
there is a block and nobody listens to your suggestion, the
strategy is fairly clear. You find out who prepares the heads

---

[1] Although many people tend to talk about induction as being concerned with
probationers only, it is actually concerned with everybody up to and including
the head of a school.

of departments' agenda and you say: 'Can I do a very brief paper, half a side of A4, on the trouble I feel I'm having in looking after students?' You might privately think you actually do it better than most of the other departments in the school. But that is not the point: you need to get the subject on the agenda in a way that does not look as if you are telling everybody else you reckon you do it better. Then I suggest you put a brief paper to your colleague heads of departments on the problems you are having and the ways in which others could possibly help you, outlining the need for the school to develop an overall policy. You might then be able to get some agreement throughout the school. As head of department you are responsible for contributing to that overall school policy, and no head of department can merely complain because the school has not got such a policy.

What are a head of department's responsibilities for students, and how can you cope with them? There are eight aspects of this part of the job.

First, you need practical liaison with the tutors in the departments from which your students come. As George Phipson pointed out (Chapter 2), a head of department must be willing to fit in with the school's overall plans, so that the school does not have to work with too many different training departments. It is bad to slip into a policy of shifting around so that you get students from different places every year, depending on which gets the letter in first to the school. The head of department must establish a proper liaison and exchange of syllabuses with the training department. I think you should be really quite fierce and refuse to take a student if his tutor does not come for a briefing on the school department before that student comes. You have the right as the head of department to refuse to take a student; you must lay down certain conditions, and that is a reasonable one.

Second, you should plan in advance of the arrival of the student what kind of programme the student might follow. It should be comparatively flexible, in that things may reveal themselves in that first discussion with the student which will make you want to alter the plan. But you should certainly have some ideas in advance. Too many students turn up at a school and the head of department sits down and says, 'Well, let's see then . . .'

Third, you should have special student documentation ready so that you do not have to fiddle around in filing cabinets for your odd bits of paper. The pack of papers may not be quite the same as given to probationary teachers or to new teachers, but it should cover the department and the school comprehensively.

Fourth, you should plan a certain amount of variety for the student. You should make sure he is attached to a pastoral group (a tutor group), and has a taste of different aspects of the work of the department and of the school. That must include observation of other departments.

Fifth, I consider that each student should have a main teacher to whom he is attached, who acts as the main mentor and guide. This person may not necessarily be the head of department. (There are schools where the head of department takes students on the grounds that he has so much work to do it is best to have a student so that he has time for the lessons. That is, of course, totally unprofessional. Indeed taking a student properly is more exhausting and time-consuming than not taking one!)

Sixth, the head of department must keep general oversight, and it is a good idea in a large department to have a planning session with the main teachers in advance, and for each to learn from the other about how to handle the task.

Seventh, I believe that students should take over classes bit by it. It is not really helpful to throw all the problems at somebody simultaneously. Giving somebody class control, lesson planning, discipline, exposition, and so forth, all at once does not make that person a competent teacher. Rather, you should work as a partner with that student, and hand over certain bits on certain days: one day the student might merely collect up the homework; another day he might wait until you have started the lesson and only then take over.

Finally, the eighth point: you should make sure the student is given experience over the whole range of school activities. This includes supervisory duties, and the social and cultural activities of the school.

Induction

Again, there really should be a school policy for the induction of new teachers. It is very difficult for a head of department to 'go it alone' on this. A number of schools lay on a proper course for new teachers. When I was at Woodberry Down School it used to be two days in the summer holidays. Whether those new teachers were coming in as heads of departments or as probationers, the course was run by the senior teacher for in-service training, and included sessions with the caretaker and school secretary, sessions on the structure of the school, pastoral care, and the entire pattern of organization. It is quite deplorable that so many teachers have had to walk into school on the first day of term without having had a formal briefing. To be around for a couple of days at the end of a summer term is no substitute for methodically covering what needs to be known. It is a good idea, but not a sufficient preparation to visit a school and to be around and to observe. There should be a proper induction. There may be somebody outside your department with a general responsibility for probationers, some kind of professional tutor. There is always a difficult responsibility balance here. Should the head of department hand over to the professional tutor, or should the head of department keep it all to himself? This balance has to be worked out on a school-wide basis, and I think some overlap does not matter. The school-based general tutor should take responsibilities for general school matters, and the head of department tackle points nearer to the departmental focus.

When does this induction programme start? It should start the morning after the appointment meeting. That is the time when there should be a letter from the head of department, the initial sending of documentation, and the initial setting up of personal contacts. It may be difficult if your new teacher is in a different part of the country. But there must be some way of keeping up the information from then onwards. One or two things are quite simple: for instance, supposing the appointment was made for September, one simple mechanical thing to do is to ensure that the minutes and agendas of all subsequent departmental meetings and staff meetings are sent to the new teacher. They will not all make absolute sense to the new teacher, but they will begin to fill in the picture.

Pre-term is most important — that period before the pupils come in and before the school is too frantic. This is the time when a calm, fairly formal, methodical covering of the departmental structure, the set lists, the pupil records and the syllabus should be fitted in. It is helpful, particularly for a probationer, to have these things done a few days before term starts.

What are the needs of a probationer? Perhaps they are so obvious they hardly need stressing.

He must have information on the geography of the school. It is sometimes difficult to get to know the layout of a school, and I think it is best to have a formal plan. (I often wonder why as educators, we are so unwilling to do things for each other that we should think necessary for pupils. If it is a complex, multi-site building with a complicated numbering system, it is perfectly easy to have this laid out on a clear map that can be given to new teachers.)

The new teacher should also have an outline of the broad

educational philosophy of the school, and he should know in advance what he is expected to do apart from his timetabled teaching. (This, incidentally, illustrates one of the ways you can work as a head of department: if you find that you have senior staff who are not making things clear to new teachers, you can say to the head: 'I am in some difficulty, because I wouldn't want to usurp your position and I don't want to speak on my own to my new teachers about the general aims and methods of the school. It would be terribly helpful if you could do a document for the new teachers.' It is very difficult for a head to say no in these circumstances, and in that way you will gradually start altering things.) The new teacher also needs to familiarize himself with the teaching methods of the department. He must be clear about the disciplinary support system that operates, and what he should do in an emergency. He will need advice, criticism and encouragement, and he should know where to turn for this.

All new teachers bring something with them. They do not come merely as blank sheets that have to be impressed with what goes on in the school. One of the head of department's first tasks is to find out the particular strengths and interests of the new teachers, so that they can be given some way of flourishing very early. It gives them great confidence if they are recognized as having some particular contribution to make. It is one of the good things about a comprehensive school, that there is a comprehensive staff. There is always somebody with some special interest. With the new teacher this needs to be drawn out as early as possible in his time at the school.

During the year you must ensure that new teachers are briefed before certain events come up, such as parents' evenings. If a probationary teacher has had only the usual initial training, he may never have attended a parents' evening and it is obviously helpful if he is given a briefing. I used to feel it was somewhat arrogant to tell well-educated, adult, independent people how to do things. I now feel it is arrogant not to. To suggest that if you explain just how a parents' evening will be, and what you recommend (not to forget to take the pupils' work along, and so forth) it is going to cramp the new teacher, who is then going to follow what you say slavishly — this is actually to be so arrogant as to think each teacher has no individuality. It is better to explain and not take anything for granted.

The head of department should keep an eye on the calendar of the year, and the timing of key events. For instance, if reports are going to have to be written in so many weeks' time, new teachers need careful advance warning. Lesson observation seems to me to be vital at an early stage. The methods are described in Chapter 5. I wish merely to emphasize that the head of department should not leave this too late, maybe on the grounds that the new teachers need to find their feet. The new teachers may not be finding their feet at all, they may be really getting into trouble.

The head of department should offer support, if necessary by removing difficulties. I do not see why a new teacher should have to face the notorious X, who is calculated to ruin any lesson in three minutes flat. There seems little reason why that particular professional challenge should not be kept back for a year from the probationer if it is at all possible to remove X to the head of department's own class or that of some other experienced teacher.

It is better for a head of department not to be over-generous and euphorically optimistic in what he says in judgement of a probationer's performance. Of course, the head of department wants to be hopeful and encouraging. Looking back over some of the probationary forms I have written over recent years, and the notes that heads of departments have given me to help write them, I think there has too often been a rather romantic, glowing optimism which has been counterproductive. If that first assessment for the probationary report hides the reality of serious difficulties, and masks how far the teacher has to travel on the journey towards sure classroom management, the new teacher has not been helped in any real way. Indeed, it can then become harder to have the frank, technical discussion that is required. The senior staff in the school have not been alerted to the problem; nor has the teacher himself. Of course, it is depressing for the probationer to know that his first weeks were awful, but it isolates the teacher with his problem if they really were awful, but the head of department says: 'Marvellous! marvellous! Don't worry it will all be fine.' It is better to try to face reality, as sympathetically and constructively as possible.

Responsibilities and planning

A department has to distribute responsibilities.[1] It must also undertake medium- and long-term planning. Both these needs can be seen not only as ends in themselves, but also as ways of helping yourself as head of department and your team develop professional knowledge and skills.

[1] Discussed in Michael Marland, *Head of Department* (Heinemann Educational Books, 1971), Chapter 2, 'The complementary team'.

Departmental meeting

The departmental meeting, for instance, is a most important in-service training instrument; most of us got most of our in-service training through the departmental meeting. If that meeting is run properly as a professional forum, not merely a confused mixture of notices, exhortations and vague philosophy, it can serve as a seminar as well as an executive event. (Appendix 1 gives brief notes on running such meetings.) The most important point is that items on the agenda should have a clear function: review ('How did the new scheme in the third year go this year?'), exploration ('What do you really feel about a craft department which is going to have girls coming into it for the first time?') and planning ('How are we going to set the third year next year?') are separate functions. It is very difficult to get this right. One of the reasons why meetings in schools are often irritating to a point of distressing tension is that they frequently get these functions confused. Sometimes it is not really quite clear whether the meeting is discussing the social conditions in the area, the fundamental ideas of comprehensive education, or an analysis of why the internal examination arrangements were such a muddle last week; whether in fact the meeting is to plan something; or whether it is a briefing on something that has already been planned. In a briefing meeting there is no real space for new ideas, for that is not the time to have any fundamental discussions, which should have been had earlier.

There needs to be a balance of the different kinds of meeting items. Some of them must be proper professional exploration, and different members of the team should be given the responsibility for introducing particular topics. One colleague can prepare a brief paper, and speak to it, on the problems of reading in the mathematics department, for example, or another may speak on the problems of discussion in science. The head of department should not necessarily choose his deputy, or even the most experienced person, but anybody who is going to give the topic a little bit of thought and introduce it helpfully. This is not only very good professional development for the individual, but also makes the ensuing discussion much better, because it has been focused.

Curriculum planning

Next, there is curriculum planning, which can also be seen as part of professional development. Proper curriculum planning requires those concerned to do adequate homework.

That homework can be spread out around the team, so that, for instance, one teacher can be given responsibility for looking at one aspect of the existing syllabus and making a critique of it. Then there is drafting a paper, which I consider one of the most valuable kinds of in-service training that there is. It is one thing to contribute views in a discussion, but quite another to have to polish those views so that they can be a positive contribution, and will be open to other people to comment on. Unfortunately there are many people in teaching who sound off pretty elaborately at various kinds of meetings, but when you say, 'Well, would you like just to jot those ideas down for the next meeting?', they are unable to. (It must be added that this task frightens some people, and if you are yourself fairly adept at drafting, you may overlook the terrifying task you have given a colleague. Some teachers have done so little writing in their professional career that they are really unable to do it, and therefore need some help. Of course, giving that help is in fact giving professional development help also.)

Selection of learning material

Then there is the selection of learning materials. This is discussed from the point of view of a reading policy in Chapter 9. It also, though, has its in-service component. How do you select learning materials? There are considerable doubts about how it is carried out,[1] but at its best it also can be seen as professional development. British educational autonomy is pointless if it is not well used. The fact that we can choose our own material in schools is pointless, and we might as well have it selected by the state or by the county council, if in fact we are not going to select the material methodically, and really use the full range for selection. A start can be made by writing to the publishers, something which is very rarely done.[2] It is best to send a circular letter, saying the department wants material suitable for, for instance, a first-year mixed-ability class on primitive architecture, and would the publisher please send anything they may have which they wish the department to consider. Usually publishers will send only what has been asked for. The packages will then start arriving, and you can hand them around the department in various ways. You can put a label on each and let different

[1] The Centre for User Studies at Sheffield University has published a methodical study: Kate Vincent, *A Survey of the Methods by Which Teachers Select Books*, CRUS Occasional Paper no. 3, 1980, British Library Research and Development Department Report no. 5549.

[2] The easiest method is to write to the Director of the Educational Publishers Council, 19 Bedford Square, London, WC1; they will ensure that all member publishers are circulated.

people see them, and ask for their comments, or you can put one particular teacher in charge of one particular field. In these ways material selection is very good for career development.

Division of responsibilities

In the introduction the division of responsibilities was noted as one of the tasks in structuring the team. Obviously you mainly need to look at this from the point of view of making the team work. However, the dividing of responsibilities can also be looked at from the point of view of career development.

It is amazing how many departments ask for an extra responsibility post, or want as many posts as they can get in the department, merely to encourage the teachers, or even perhaps departmental aggrandizement, not because they have any view of the responsibility structure in the department. Many departments have difficulties simply because the head of department is overworked, and it is not quite clear how the head of department can delegate, because there is not a proper structure through which to do it. For instance, often in large science departments, for historic reasons there is a head of biology, a head of physics, and a head of chemistry. Despite the fact that there may be integrated science for the first two or three years and general science for the less able in the fourth and fifth years, and that there is not very much separate chemistry being taught, there may still be a head of chemistry on a high salary scale. The function of that head of chemistry needs very careful looking at. Presumably one function is to provide advice on the chemistry element in general science, but that may be the limit of his tasks. Looking at the structure from the point of view of the full range of departmental responsibilities, it is very easy to find many large schools where the head of the science department, with a staff of maybe nine scientists and with 1500 pupils, is carrying most of the burden of looking after the teachers (the biggest head of department burden), and most of the burden of looking after the difficult pupils, because there is not a delegating structure. Or there may be a mathematics department with a head and a deputy and a sprinkling of Scale 2s. It may not be at all clear what these Scale 2 people are doing. The head of department cannot be paid any more, or given more hours in the day; the only thing that can be done to help that head of department is to put a proper structure underneath him. This means looking at the relationship of the jobs within the department.

What is the job of deputy? With a bit of luck the deputy will rarely have to deputize. Deputies do not have to do very much deputizing. What do they do? Frequently it is not at all clear, and that vagueness sets the pattern for the rest of the team. How then should you divide up responsibilities? There is no way of carving them up which does not produce an artificial division, but nevertheless it has to be done. There are four main ways you can divide up responsibilities, which I call 'territory', 'aspect', 'pupils' and 'teachers'.

By 'territory' I mean that there might in fact be some divisions in certain departments by architectural parts of the school: the upper floor, the north wing, or the other site. By 'aspect', I mean a part or facet of the subject. It may in a craft department be metalwork, or it may be design. By 'pupils', I naturally mean a group of the pupils, but the division may be horizontally, by year, or vertically, by section. Some schools do it by examination entry. The CSE pupils then go to this person and the O-level pupils to another. I am unhappy with that, for although it makes examination entry checking easier, it is otherwise an artificial split. Finally, there is division by teachers: are all the teachers in theory responsible directly to the head of department, and is he responsible for all of them? This may work in a department of three, but what about in an English department with, say, eight full-timers and about the same number of part-timers? Is the head of department to be directly responsible for the whole team?

Those, then, are my four main dividing principles: territory, aspect, pupils and teachers. A department will have to use more than one of those principles, but care is needed so that they do not conflict with each other.

Consider, for instance, division by pupil. Are you going to divide them by years, by houses or by category? I am not very happy about dividing them horizontally; in fact, I think there are serious snags in dividing responsibilities horizontally. One of the greatest weaknesses in curriculum planning in our schools is sequencing. There is a distinct lack of what the Americans call 'vertical articulation'. In many schools what is done in the first three years is a sort of marking time. The science department which says that the pupils cannot understand chemistry in the fourth year, and cannot read the chemistry textbook, often has not seen that there are no textbooks used at all in years one and two, because there has not been sequencing up the years. That lack is one of the main disadvantages if you hand out your responsibilities on too much of a horizontal basis. For that reason I am not very happy about division by examination entries either. It may seem convenient to have a deputy in charge of CSE and for the head of department to stay in charge of O level. It makes the clerical side of examination entries easy, but it does *not* make the relationship between the syllabus in the lower part of the school and the work in those examination forms easy. I would therefore stress the need to create vertical continuity.

One of the classic ways of producing divisions is to give subordinates responsibilities for two different vertical threads — one for the vertical thread of pupils. In a house-based school this is very easy. In fact I have known quite a few departments where there have been two co-deputies, one responsible for a pair or three houses, and the other responsible for the other houses, with the advantage that the two deputies know exactly which pupils they are responsible for, and the pupils know who is responsible for them. However, I consider that that responsibility has to be balanced with an aspect of the curriculum also. Sometimes this may be done horizontally — for example, having someone looking at the first-year lower-school science, or the introductory year of the second modern language. But I have already recommended that curriculum responsibilities should also have a vertical thread, with somebody responsible for a particular aspect of the work up the years, whether it is something as small as photography or something as large as literature. In a large departmental team, it helps also if the teacher teams are divided up, so that scale-post holders are responsible for sub-teams of teachers. It is particularly important for the extra-departmental teachers, those who come into the department from other specialist departments for a class or two. They need more discussion and planning time to prepare their work than the full-time teachers, and it is good to divide responsibility for them between your subordinates.

Thus a set of responsibilities is built up from an inter-connected set of responsibilities, probably linking pupils and teachers (perhaps with territorial responsibilities) on the one hand with curriculum strands on the other.

When a job is devised, or even as an aid to devising it, a description in the form of a 'job specification' must be drawn up. Appendix 4 is one such example — with the tasks analysed person by person. An alternative approach is to draw a grid with a series of boxes. Along the top each column is labelled with an aspect of the work of the department (e.g. assessment, syllabus planning, materials). The various teachers taking responsibility are listed down the side. The specific tasks (and the pupils to whom the tasks are related) are then indicated in the boxes. This presentation does not merely tell you what each person is responsible for, but allows you to see who is responsible for each aspect of the work. It is also particularly good at showing how the responsibilities are inter-related, something which is not at all clear from a simple person-by-person list.

As well as the formal scale-post responsibility structure, I consider it wise for all teachers who are mainly members of the departmental team to have some responsibility, whether or not recognized by scale posts. This is an accepted tradition in many schools, but there are others where the legacy of reorganization and difficulties of management have led to a 'leave-it-to-those-who-are-paid' attitude. This is not only bad for the overall work of the department, but also unfortunate for the young teacher, whose career development can be so substantially enhanced by having some specific responsibility.

Finally, there is the problem of briefing and guidance. No one's professional development will be helped by undertaking responsibilities which are ill-defined. Every teacher deserves a proper briefing. It is dangerously easy to presume that what is required is obvious. That can lead to disappointment all round. It is both safer in practical terms, and better in personal development terms, to make sure that as head of department you go over the detailed job specification with your colleague, and allow him the opportunity to inquire, to comment and, if necessary, to negotiate.

Specific in-service work

The previous section considered utilizing the necessary planning work of a departmental team as a vehicle for career development. Now we come to what is more specific in-service training. 'Inset' is an ugly word, but its meaning is clear: in-service education and training. The primary task of the head of department is for school-focused in-service work. 'School-focused' in-service training does not mean *where* that in-service training is carried out, or even *who* carries it out, but that the school as a client, or in this case the head of department or the departmental team as a client, has articulated its needs and drawn up a plan for trying to meet those needs. The Department of Education and Science booklet, *Making INSET Work*,[1] puts the requirements like this:

1   Identify the main needs
2   Decide on and implement the general programme
3   Evaluate the effectiveness of this general programme
4   Follow up the ideas gained.

These are four simple phrases outlining a programme of

[1] DES, 1978.

school-focused in-service training, but in fact few programmes
ever get that much completed. However, it is very valuable if
a department asks itself: 'How are we as a department? What
are our weaknesses? What do we want to build up? What
kind of programme of in-service work do we want?' Instead
most departments have a fragmentary in-service training
pattern, in which people go for odd courses, for days or
terms, and do not report back. That is not to say that there
should be no purely individual in-service training, for there
will always be a need for that. However, there must be an
articulated departmental programme in which you say:
'This is what we have been attempting; what more do we
want to do?'

What form might this in-service department-focused training and education take? Of course it might take the form of
suggesting a teacher goes on an existing course. Perhaps it
will in some cases mean persuading someone to go to a particular lecture and bring back a brief résumé. Certainly it is
important to make sure that your department is being informed of courses available; that you keep a notice-board
with details of external courses; that the staff actually go
through them as a department and select from them — and
that they are followed up. If any of us go on a course in
school time or with school money, surely there should be
some feedback to the other people who did not have that
privilege.

The use of existing courses for the needs of the team will
entail more than facilitating choice and encouraging colleagues to make use of the details offered. More substantially
it may mean analysing the needs of the department, and
seeing who is willing to try to get secondment to go on a
long course, or even take an Open University degree. In other
words, a department can use *external* in-service work for
department-focused purposes if it shops around carefully
enough. In one example, for instance, a deputy head of house
from a London school was sent to a course in Lancashire on
pastoral care, because that course was covering an aspect
relevant to particular needs of the school. There is clearly
plenty of scope for the internal use of externally-provided
in-service work.

The next element in a programme is seminars run in
the school by the department (or they may be larger than
the department and include other people as well). These
seminars can be run by your own staff or visitors. Do not
overlook your own staff. In the school there may be someone who is really a great expert on a needed topic, but
his job in the school may not make his expertise known.

There are others, more obviously, who are designated as the teacher 'in charge of' a particular aspect, and whose expertise is thus advertised. Visitors can be advisers, whether they come from colleges of education, your LEA, or elsewhere. Frustratingly, if you have identified a major problem in your school it is probably a major problem precisely because teachers do not know much about it, and that in turn is because those who trained them initially were not very experienced either! Therefore the expertise for the most serious common gaps is not very easy to bring in from the local colleges. Nevertheless, it is often there, and these people will come in as part of the college in-service budget of hours.

If the LEA has an in-service training budget, it is frequently possible to get part of it to pay someone to come into the school. At the least you can probably get their expenses from the school fund. Such outside visitors can be very valuable *if you brief them properly*. Do not simply say, 'Come in and do a session!' Tell them exactly where your department stands. Obviously you will not want to tie them down so that they cannot be themselves, but tell them carefully what you think your team needs.

In all this, do not forget to use inspectors and advisers, from Inspectorate and LEA. HMI very rarely say no to coming to help a school on some matter or other, and I would think that they are an important under-used facility. We tend to look on those in the inspectorate and the advisory service as people who choose to come in when they want to. In an autonomous school system they are the servants of the schools; and are only too pleased to come in and give assistance if they are briefed.

Colleagues from other schools, perhaps in the same LEA can be very stimulating, either as main speakers, or as group leaders. (For instance, in one Oxfordshire school's programme for a day's course, each discussion group was led by an experienced teacher from another school.)

When will sessions like this be held? After school is the traditional time. But there are other ways. The DES 1959 School Regulations are quite clear on the matter of school closures. Full-time school education is defined as requiring 400 sessions, from which 20 sessions may be taken for 'occasional closures'. If you work in an area where the occasional closures have always been taken as regular holidays, there are difficulties as it is literally illegal to take any more occasional closures. Most LEAs in fact keep a pool or a reserve of occasional closures for the very reasons that the regulations foresaw. If your authority is not using all those days, it is possible to ask for them. Obviously, you cannot have an occasional closure just for one department. But it might be possible to persuade your other colleagues to have a day of departmental in-service work across the school.

Another way of getting time, though one which is not always very popular with colleagues, is to ask the person who does the absence cover to cover your department fully for a day or half a day some time towards the end of the summer term. Some departments use weekends, and this is especially valuable if the education authority will use part of its in-service budget to pay for a residential weekend. That is the very best way I know of getting powerfully effective in-service training for a department.

Finally, there are departments that use a day of 'their own time' in the holidays. When it is arranged, this is very much appreciated, as it is really rewarding to have a day's work with your colleagues on some topic which you think is valuable, when you have no worries about tomorrow, and when you are feeling relaxed and fresh.

The most important aspect of within-school seminars is choosing the topic and planning the approach. What kind of topics might these seminars have? I suggest that they be fairly narrowly focused. They should only rarely be something huge like 'Education in modern society', or 'Preparation for the world today'. They should relate to a sequence of thinking, they should grow out of perceived needs, and should have follow-up. They should be relevant to the needs of the department, and they should if possible be practical. Whenever possible something should come out of them: if you come away from a weekend seminar having drafted a policy statement, you really have done something and learned a great deal as well. Thus an end-product is always valuable. There are times when the seminar should be background, when what you want your department to do is to hear somebody and talk with somebody who is not actually going to help with next week's lessons, or even next term's schemes, but is going to invigorate the background thinking. There are other times when the focus should be as narrow as a single lesson, a single topic, or a single skill.

Such seminars need proper pre-documentation, and it is very helpful to have discussion on study material, such as extracts from textbooks, extracts from pupils' work, and tape-recordings, so that the function of the seminar can arise from concentrating on the piece of material. Then the arguments are close to specifics rather than touching on grandiose general philosophy.

Career development

All that I have said so far has been concerned with more than the working of the department; it has been directed at the underlying career development of each individual teacher. However, this work cannot be left merely implicit, and a brief consideration of the specific needs of career development is important.

The head of department is responsible for assisting his individual teachers to think about their long-term career. How will they be if they are still teaching the same syllabus to the same kind of classes in another ten years? Do not let this become a nightmare for the teacher after those ten years, but help teachers think about it bit by bit. Some people are good at going on doing the same thing for ever; other people go stale on the job. Once in a while, you need to have a formal interview with teachers. If you are close to a member of your team, it is doubly important that once a year or so you find a framework for a discussion which is more than an informal chat. There are various ways of setting up this framework: one is to say, 'Can we fix a time to go somewhere outside the departmental headquarters and talk about each aspect of your work'. Another way is to create a social occasion with a different context for the discussion, so that you are able to get away from the things you normally talk about, and concentrate on more difficult long-term things.

Senior staff should be kept informed of the work of your teachers. A headteacher cannot be expected — particularly in a largish school — to notice every good thing done by every teacher. Make sure that you alert the head to that good work.

Ensure that the teaching timetable of your team has an eye not only to the expediency of this term, this year and next September, but to career development also. Are there certain topics or certain types of classes that a teacher has not taught that he would like to? Have some teachers never done sixth-form work, but have been a bit too shy to ask for it? Have they never taught less able children, but actually might be rather good with them? Are there other subjects in the school that they ought to teach? Keep your ear close to the ground. I blame the head of department who does not spot these kinds of things, for it is one way of developing someone professionally by altering, changing, adding to their teaching timetable and their jobs.

To do this you will have to visit lessons in the way that Peter Stokes describes (Chapter 5). These visits should not be limited to the new teacher. Indeed, it is very much the teacher who has been with the department for ten years and does not look like moving whose lessons are never observed, but who probably needs observation and analysis most. Part of the value of such visits lies in what can be fed back into the work of others, but part lies in meeting the need of that teacher to have his work recognized as essential to the work of the school. If you do not observe his lessons, you cannot provide the feedback and praise necessary to help further develop professional skills and confidence.

Professional reading

It seems strange, but it is also necessary in covering aspects of in-service professional development, to insist on the importance of professional reading. Sadly this is neglected by many ambitious teachers, and their ignorance is sometimes revealed at interviews for promotion. When that is so, the head of department must take some blame. He can help by providing reading lists, subscribing to journals, and by setting up a regular reporting session, in which colleagues report on journal articles and books read. Every department should certainly have a departmental professional library, and this can be supplemented by loans from the county library, or by hiring one of the excellent National Book League exhibitions.[1] These range across many different aspects of education, and some are devoted to selections of pupil material.

Summary

The argument of this chapter is that there are many informal and formal ways in which a head of department can show recognition of the fact that there is a need for professional development, and that, from the specific needs of INSET to the less tangible aspects of personal growth, there is a need for information, planning, support and the giving of real responsibilities. Indeed, helping your teachers develop their own professional skills is one of the major ways of helping your own development as head of department. Your task is to create nourishment through continuity, and to ensure that the department is not only teaching, but that it is learning as well.

[1] Write for a catalogue to National Book League, Touring Exhibitions Department, Book House, Wandsworth, London, SW18.

5 Monitoring the work of teachers
Peter Stokes

Newly appointed heads of department are usually well qualified with good teaching experience and a real determination
to succeed. Self-confidence is often another characteristic
of successful applicants for head of department posts, and at
the moment of appointment and promotion I suspect many
of them enter into a state of euphoria. This condition prevails until new colleagues and new situations are encountered
when the new post is taken up and then reality replaces
euphoria. Realization dawns that the main task of a head of
department is to lead a group of teachers, a disparate collection of individuals, without whose co-operation and good-
will success cannot be achieved.

It is not enough to be an excellent teacher, an enthusiast
for the subject, a good administrator and an original thinker.
The head of department will stand or fall by his ability to
create a team effort which will be capable of achieving the
aims and objectives of the department. If this ability is
properly used, years of success based on the satisfying
experience of leadership of a lively, effective department
will follow. If the ability is lacking or is ineffectively used,
a period of increasing frustration and disillusionment will
result.

Leadership of teachers is the key. There are a number of
factors upon which good leadership depends and one of these,
in my view, is the recognition of the need to monitor the
work of the teachers and of course the ability to implement
skilfully a monitoring programme. A good head of department would not hesitate to evaluate all other resources
available to him: textbooks, reference books, worksheets,
audio/visual equipment and materials, accommodation,
furniture, etc. He would examine them and their effectiveness in the light of the aims and objectives of the department, but I believe that many heads of department baulk
at the task of monitoring the effectiveness of their colleagues.
Yet the teacher is the most vital resource in any department.

The effectiveness of the team of teachers is the most important deciding factor as to whether the department will succeed
or fail. This reluctance to monitor is understandable, however,
for when we attempt it we enter a highly sensitive area – the
minefield of professional relationships. It is a minefield, however, that can be negotiated, and the first step is to be clear
as to the need for monitoring.

Reasons for monitoring

Monitoring should give a head of department knowledge and
understanding of the teachers who work in the department.
It should enable the head of department to assess the strengths
and weaknesses of the teachers in his team. With this knowledge and understanding it should be possible to:

1 Decide upon the overall strategy for the department – the
   aims and objectives a head of department sets must be
   dependent, to a large extent, upon the capabilities and
   competencies of the teachers in the team.

   (a) Can mixed-ability teaching be attempted (if there is
       choice) and to which pupils and at what levels?
   (b) Will the department be able to tackle Mode III schemes?
   (c) Is team teaching a possibility?
   (d) How should the teachers in the team be deployed?
       Who should teach the sixth form? Who should tackle
       other examination work? What age-groups and/or
       ability groups should each teacher cover?
   (e) Is the 'advisory' system for allocation of departmental
       tasks (as outlined in Michael Marland's book, *Head of
       Department*[1]) to be used? If so, monitoring is essential.

2 Form a professional judgement about teachers in the
   department, which may be needed for three purposes:

   (a) The head teacher will need to know when he has to
       write confidential reports on teachers seeking a move
       for promotion or any other reason.
   (b) The head of department may need to make recom-
       mendations to the head regarding internal promotions
       within his department.
   (c) The head of department will be able to advise the head
       as to what type of teacher (in terms of specialisms and
       interests) is required if a replacement is needed in the
       department.

[1] Heinemann Educational Books, 1971.

3 Make an appreciation of the training needs of the department personnel as a whole and for each individual teacher. The head of department can:

(a) Plan an in-service training programme covering such items as:

    (i) preparation of worksheets
    (ii) setting of examination questions
    (iii) teaching of mixed-ability groups
    (iv) teaching slow learners
    (v) use of new resources and methods.

(b) Bring the in-service training needs of the department to the notice of the advisory services of the local education authority.

(c) Bring out the individual skills that are in the team in such a way that the whole team can benefit from them.

(d) Decide on a programme of support and guidance for the under-performing teacher in the team.

4 Deal with the personal and professional growth of the individual teacher in the department:

(a) Advise individual teachers regarding further training and thus:

    (i) fill gaps in knowledge and expertise
    (ii) remove weaknesses in techniques.

(b) Discuss the place of the teacher in the department and change the role if necessary to that the teacher obtains the right kind of experience.

What areas of the teachers' work can be monitored?

1 General efficiency in administration (mark lists, gradings, examination questions) — are the tasks done efficiently and completed on time? Punctuality to school, to lessons, to meetings. General reliability.

2 Record book -- is this well kept and regularly handed in? Is it a fair record of the work done by the groups taught? Does it serve its purpose? Does it ensure that the teacher plans his time properly?

3 Is appropriate homework set in accordance with the agreed timetable and is the pupils' work regularly and properly marked?

4 Examination results — internal and external. How do they compare with the reasonable expectation of performance for the groups taught, and with results in previous years?

5 Knowledge of pupils taught — by the half-year point can the teacher give a short but clear account of each pupil's potential and progress?
6 Writing reports on pupils — are these perceptive and so written that they are helpful to pupils and parents?
7 Contribution to departmental meetings — is it generally positive, producing ideas, or is it usually negative, stressing difficulties and emphasizing complaints?
8 Classroom teaching.

Monitoring classroom teaching

Before we examine the monitoring of this area of a teacher's work it would be as well to sound a cautionary note. It is essential in the process of monitoring that the relationship between the head of department and teacher should not be damaged. Monitoring should be constructive in its effect. If it is badly implemented, it can be positively destructive of the work of the department, for it will lower the morale of the staff and antagonize them. George Cooke, County Education Officer for Lincolnshire, in a recent article on the assessment of a teacher's performance sounded a warning note:

> We are now busy opening up the 'secret garden' of the curriculum to public scrutiny and public accountability, but there is still a small area in education which can never be fully shared by those outside it — the area of the relationships between the teacher and the taught when no one else is around. This in qualitative terms is the area that really matters. Here the individual teacher is potentially most effective but also most isolated and vulnerable. Here most of all he needs to be confident in his skills and relationships; in sympathy with the aims and ethos of the school and aware (especially if things get rough) that he is part of a team and able to rely fully in every reasonable action on the support of those 'higher up', and it is precisely here that external judgements and measurements, though not without their importance, are most uncertain.
>
> The special teacher/pupil relationships in the 'secret area' are inevitably changed by the presence of a third party. We do well to remember that in teaching there are a thousand and one ways to the Kingdom of God and that many of the greatest teachers have been thoroughly unorthodox in their methods but at the same time despite (or more probably because of) their unorthodoxy, supremely effective. Most of us can remember vividly those teachers who were different from the average because they really stimulated our interest and eagerness to learn. I can certainly recall a number of teachers who, measured by any standard test, would come out rather badly but who would come out very well indeed if judged in terms of what long-term effects they had on their pupils, how far they inspired in them the pursuit of truth and beauty, how much they raised their

confidence, their expectation of achievement and their determination to set the world to rights.[1]

These words should act as a caution but not a prohibition.

The exercise of leadership in this area needs to be skilfully and delicately carried out. There are many styles of leadership and it would be difficult to suggest a model approach for the head of department. However, the right atmosphere must be created in the department by its head. There must be a climate of opinion which will make possible the acceptability of monitoring. The head of department must show that he trusts his staff and that he is supportive of their efforts. He must make it clear why he needs to know what his teachers are doing. He should openly discuss it in departmental meetings and invite suggestions regarding the implementation of monitoring. If his leadership is good, teachers will accept the monitoring of their work, even in that most sensitive of areas, that of classroom teaching. Teachers must trust the head of department. They must know that there will be private discussion of what has been observed with the opportunity for them to put their point of view.

Having acknowledged the difficulties, however, one should not draw back from the task of assessing practical teaching in the classroom. It is essential that the head of department does this for the probationers who become members of the department from time to time, and also for new members of staff who join the department. It should also be seen as essential for the head of department to observe every member of the department teaching at some time or other during the school year.

The observer must not judge on impression. If he enters a colleague's classroom his approach should be on the highest professional level. Some teachers object because they believe the observer is not prepared for observation, that he is too casual. He should not 'pop in and out' on excuses. It should be done properly. The following list of criteria is one way of approaching the task. The teacher should be given this in advance of the observation and it should be fully discussed afterwards.

Criteria for the assessment of practical teaching

1 Relationship with pupils:
   (a) Atmosphere of classroom

[1] George Cooke in *Education*, vol. 152, no. 2, 14 July 1978. (Reproduced by kind permission of the author.)

   (b) Responsiveness and co-operation of pupils
   (c) Consideration of pupils' individual problems

2 Preparation:
   (a) Adequacy of lesson notes
   (b) Suitability of lesson content to age and ability of pupils
   (c) Teacher's knowledge of subject

3 Classroom organization:
   (a) Arrangement and distribution of materials
   (b) Use of space, equipment and teaching aids
   (c) Organization and planning for group and individual activities
   (d) Marking and display of pupils' work

4 Class control:
   (a) Ability to establish suitable conditions for learning to take place
   (b) Ability to secure and retain pupils' attention
   (c) Anticipation and avoidance of disorderly behaviour
   (d) Firmness and consistency when required

5 Communication with pupils:
   (a) Clarity and audibility of voice
   (b) Appropriateness of vocabulary
   (c) Awareness of pupils' linguistic needs
   (d) Success in communicating with pupils

6 Effective use of teacher's personality and expertise:
   (a) Ability to arouse interest and enthusiasm of pupils
   (b) Degree and purposefulness of pupils' activity
   (c) Progression of learning sequences
   (d) Initiative and resourcefulness

Almost inevitably monitoring will reveal some inadequacies, or deficiencies, or under-performance in the teacher's work. What should be done when these come to light? In the majority of cases, a word of advice, some guidance, or a suggestion to try a new approach, will probably put matters right. However, there may well be cases of more serious under-performance that the head of department will have to deal with. In such cases it would be advisable to follow a consistent approach.

1 The teacher's attention should first be drawn informally to the ways in which his performance is deficient. This will

probably best be achieved by the head of department meeting in private with the teacher to discuss the inadequacies of the teacher's work and related problems.

2 Clear guidance should be given to the teacher as to what is expected of him in the future, and it will often be useful to prepare written notes of guidance giving practical advice on classroom methods, lesson planning, or whatever the particular problem may be. If the problem appears to stem from inadequate training, the head of department may be able to suggest some suitable means of further training within the school, or by attendance at in-service courses, or by visits to other schools. Advice could also be sought from the advisory team of the local education authority. Whatever form of help and support is decided upon, it is essential that a programme should be devised for the teacher, setting specific goals to be achieved over a period of time, aimed at bringing about improvements in the teacher's work.

3 It will probably be necessary for the head of department to supervise directly the teacher who is experiencing difficulties. The progress of the teacher should be carefully monitored for a reasonable period (not less than a term) and the head of department should arrange for practical support to be given through guidance, periodical meetings, discussion of progress and similar means.

4 If, after at least one term's support and supervision, the head of department is satisfied that progress is being made, the programme of support may be modified or terminated and the teacher informed accordingly. In this way many of the difficulties will be resolved, but the key to it is the acceptance, by the teacher, of the head of department's assessment of his work. Thus the informal meeting to discuss inadequacies is crucial. This meeting is likely to go well if the teacher is convinced by the head of department's approach that he is sympathetic and supportive. If, however, the teacher feels threatened or aggrieved when his inadequacies are pointed out and discussed, then it may prove very difficult for the head of department to bring about an improvement.

5 In most cases, if the guidance and support given has been appropriate, the teacher's performance will be improved, but occasionally there may be exceptions. The head of department may be confronted with the problem of the lazy teacher or the incompetent teacher who proves to be incapable of improvement. These cases are fortunately rare, but nevertheless they do exist and must therefore be

tackled. If, after going through the stages designed to help the under-performing teacher, there is no significant change, the head of department must warn the teacher that unless (after a further period) there is improvement the headteacher will be informed. When it becomes necessary to take the problem to the head, the head of department must ensure that he has a clear case to present. This can only be done if he is able to show that the teacher's work has been carefully monitored and that appropriate support and guidance has been given over a reasonable period of time.

It should be emphasized, however, that these very difficult cases are rare and I would like to end on a more positive, optimistic note. In most instances the under-performing teacher can be helped, and inadequacies and deficiencies can be overcome. Whatever approach the head of department chooses, the starting-point should be concerned with the confidence of the teacher. Restoration of confidence is paramount and is most likely to be achieved if the teacher feels that the head of department is sympathetic, understanding and supportive. There is a good chance that the teacher will be able to overcome difficulties if he has regained some of his confidence.

With the stress I have put on helping the under-performing teacher, it might appear that I believe that monitoring normally only reveals inadequacies in the teacher's work. In fact the contrary is true. On most occasions observations of the teacher's work will reveal good professional practice. Over the years, as a headteacher and now as an inspector, I have encountered, in the overwhelming number of cases, skill, enthusiasm, honest endeavour and real commitment to the job on the part of the teacher. Good practice is the norm — incompetence, indifference and idleness, very much the exception. Monitoring, therefore, should be seen as a powerful force for the encouragement and support of the teacher. Nothing is more conducive to the establishment of good relationships and a good atmosphere in a department than the proper recognition of competent professional work. If a head of department knows what his teachers are doing, then he is in a position to give them the praise and encouragement they deserve. Teachers are gratified when they believe a genuine interest is taken in the work they do and will respond by giving of their best. I believe it is a myth that teachers are essentially 'loners' who want to live in their own private classroom world all the time. It might have been true in the past, but today teachers will not respect a head of department who fails to take steps to know what is going on in the department. They have a real pride in their work and want to discuss it with their colleagues. They are not afraid to put their efforts under the scrutiny of a fellow professional they respect. They need to share their successes and failures on occasions with a sympathetic and understanding colleague. If monitoring is skilfully and appropriately used by the head of department, it is a creative force which will produce a professional climate that will enhance the work of every teacher in the department.

It is interesting to note also what the effect of carrying out a programme of monitoring can have on the individual head of department. It is somewhat akin to undergoing a 'know yourself' exercise. At best it can have three main results:

1 It can destroy the arrogance of the person monitoring, because an appreciation of the skills and expertise of others usually follows from observing someone work. This knowledge of the abilities of other people is a prerequisite if those in leadership are to be realistic about their own skills and abilities.
2 It can improve the skills of the person doing the monitoring, because good practice can be observed.
3 It can enhance the development of sound, professional relationships in a department.

It is my view, therefore, that the exercise of effective leadership by the head of department involves the need to assess the work of the teachers who make up the departmental team. There are clearly defined aspects of a teacher's work which can and should be monitored. However, the creation of a climate of understanding and co-operation is necessary before monitoring takes place, and the purposes of such monitoring should be explained to, and appreciated by, all members of the department. In particular, any monitoring of classroom teaching should be carried out with sensitivity and skill. Monitoring should be seen to be a means of support and encouragement for teachers. It must not be used in such a way that it is seen as a threat by them for then it becomes self-defeating. Above all, in our proper concern to make the education service more accountable, we should recognize that while assessment of the performance of teachers is an extremely difficult and sensitive business, competently and professionally tackled, it can have real long-term benefits.

6 Assessing the work of the pupils
Rory Deale

When I was at school, we had reports once a week: marks, grades, form order and comments — *and* a big one at the end of term. Assessing the pupils' work and reporting on it, has always been recognized as important, but, strangely enough, few teachers have received any training in how to make these assessments, either in initial training or, until quite recently, in in-service training either.

Let me take you back even further than my own school-days: to a young man who had just graduated from Oxbridge in 1909 and gone into public school teaching. After a few weeks, he wrote this in his diary:

> I object intensely to the mark system. It inculcates selfishness, destroys any chance of getting any co-operative spirit in a form and is thoroughly immoral . . . Every Saturday night, we have to collect all sorts of marks from other masters, scale and readjust them and produce an order which takes up about two hours of valuable time. I don't mind giving up time to any useful end, but I do resent doing so for a senseless one.[1]

Although he had been teaching only a few weeks, he had got to the heart of it. Why? Because this is the crucial issue in any question of assessment. What was the purpose of these weekly mark lists? Who wanted them? What were they used for? Why?

Assessment of your pupils produces — or should produce — evidence, information, feedback. It is hard to see how any teacher can do his job properly if he does not have this feedback. Assessment may be of a very informal kind: question and answer round the class when you are reading a poem perhaps. This may not be the kind of assessment you would write down in your mark-book, but all the time you are making judgements, assessing the class's reactions and getting feedback. If you mark a piece of homework, you are making an assessment. It may be a few words at

[1] From *A Schoolmaster's Diary*, ed. S. P. B. Mais (Grant Richards, 1918).

the end, or you may give it A+ or 19/20 or whatever — you are making a judgement of some sort on its merit, an assessment according to some sort of criterion on whatever scale you are using.

But now we come to one of the difficult bits: do you, as head of department, know *how* the other teachers in your department are making these judgements? Are they all looking for the same qualities in the work? Do some go for mechanical errors — spelling and punctuation — while others just let it all flow on unimpeded? Do some mark leniently, for encouragement, as it were, while others pride themselves on being hard men with rigorous standards, and nobody ever gets more than C+? Is this sort of thing discussed at departmental meetings? I think it should be because high standards are not set by marking low, but by teaching well. Do you operate a common policy within the department (and, indeed, within the school)?

Does it matter? I think it does. To take just one example — what does it mean to a child who moves from a class with an easy marker to a class with one of the 'hard men'? Does the child — and his parents — think that his work has suddenly deteriorated? The answer, unfortunately, in some cases is yes, they do. They may realize in time what has happened and adjust, of course, but should they have to? We are asking them to play a game of which only we know the rules. Not only do we keep them a secret, but we keep changing them as we go along.

It is common enough for schools to use a five-point grade scale, A—E, for communicating results to parents. There is nothing wrong with that, but it is almost equally common for some departments never to give an A. (English departments are the worst: 'A means perfection, and you cannot write a perfect English essay', so nobody gets A.) You can argue for that if you like, but what is not defensible, in my view, is for a school to claim to use five grades and then for one department to use four. It is fairly easy for the year tutor, or the head of department, or the head to look at all the grades from all the teachers and, by mentally noting 'old so-and-so never gives A', to 'aim off' and make a correction as he goes along. The parent, on the other hand, has one set of grades for one child and has to interpret them as best he can.

The idiosyncratic grade scales, used apparently at will by different departments (and often even by teachers within one department), the pluses and minuses and question marks added to lettered grades, succeed very often in making the school report virtually unintelligible to anyone except another teacher in that school. It is to be hoped, of course, that there will be a parents' meeting as well as a report, but surely the meeting ought to be to discuss future plans as a result of the report, and not a translation lesson.

Assessment is feedback, to the child, to the teacher and to the parent. It gives important information; monitoring of progress, of the work of different teachers in a department, of the degree to which the syllabus is being covered. It should give a 'profile' of the pupil — his strengths and weaknesses. This should help in making option choices in the third year which will, in turn, determine examination entries, sixth-form courses, entry to further and higher education and career choices. These are important decisions — quite possibly affecting the whole of a child's adult life — but are they made on rational grounds? We often criticize children for choosing, say, geography instead of history in the fourth year because 'My mate's doing geography', but what if the choice is made because he got A for geography and only B+ for history? And we, in the school, know that the history teacher never gives A, while the geography teacher dishes them out like Green Shield stamps?

It is in this sort of area, the comparability of assessments, that the head of department must think of the relationship between his department and the rest of the school. It is right that your department should be the most important in the school to you — but to the child it is one of many.

I repeat: assessment is important. It should provide feedback, information, evidence on which major decisions affecting a child's future, and the organization and running of the department, are based. I believe that educational decisions ought to be based on evidence, and the more evidence the better. Even if we cannot obtain all the information we need, partial evidence is still a help; the realization that it *is* only part of the picture is, of course, crucial and this applies many times when we consider issues of assessment and evaluation.

Fitness for purpose

If we turn now to look at some of the more technical questions in planning your assessment programme, we come back to where I started: why? The purpose of the assessment is of fundamental importance and once the purpose (or purposes) is clearly established, the actual assessment is usually much easier to plan and to carry out. You may be looking for diagnostic information, either about one child who has learning difficulties, or even about a whole class which is lagging behind; you may be concerned in curriculum evaluation; you may be assessing for 'qualifying' purposes – entry to the sixth, perhaps, or for setting; you may need to provide assessments on transition to a new school, or for school reports, or for employers, etc.

Some of these purposes may be incompatible with others; the way in which the information is given (grades, percentile ranks, percentage marks) will almost certainly be different, according to the recipient and the use which he intends to make of it. The purpose of the assessment must be made clear at the start.

Validity

Within the overall framework of 'fitness for purpose', three important concepts must be understood, the first of which is validity. A valid test is one which tests what it is meant to test. It may seem obvious that, if you set a test on physics, that is what it tests, but alas, things are rarely as simple as that. Complicating factors like speed of reading or reading age may invalidate what looks like a perfectly reasonable test. Some children will be affected more than others by these factors, even though their ability at physics may be identical. The test is not doing what it was meant to do.

There are a number of aspects to validity, of which the most important for our purposes is *content-validity*; the content of the test should be planned to match the content of the teaching that led up to it. Perhaps the idea of 'planning' is the single most useful one to get hold of. I expect most people have set tests or examinations the way I have: glanced through the textbook and chosen questions that were easy to set, as the pages are turned. It does not take much more time to plan it beforehand: to decide how much emphasis your course gives to factual knowledge and to set perhaps a short answer test on this aspect; to think of what other skills you are trying to develop – interpretation of data, possibly – and to incorporate some longer questions on that; to decide if there are aspects of the course that you cannot easily assess in an examination and to incorporate an element of continuous assessment as well, and so on. The question papers are set to match this specification and the chances of making a valid assessment are greatly increased.

Validity is the first requirement of fitness for purpose. An invalid test is useless, misleading and unfair to the children, and should be thrown away.

Reliability

Reliability is the second essential concept in assessment. It means accuracy or consistency — the extent to which the test would give the same results with the same children if they could do it again.

Of course, we can never expect to get perfect reliability in any form of educational assessment. It is essentially indirect. The child has certain knowledge, certain abilities in his head, but we can only discover what they are by asking him to perform a task: speaking, writing or a practical. Immediately we do this, the possibility of 'interference' arises. First, there are inevitable variations in the child's performance from day to day, due to an upset at home, a quarrel in the playground, etc. Then, the conditions of the test can be a factor: a room can be too stuffy for one child, but 'just right' for another. And the questions set can be a differential, too. Even if you set your test most carefully, you are unlikely to be able to set a question on everything. You could probably set another twenty or so questions that would be equally valid. You have to sample your syllabus to get an examination of reasonable length, but the particular sample you choose may for one child be from all the bits he has crammed the night before, while for another, the bits he is shaky on. The assessment method is another factor: some people hate multiple-choice tests, others loathe writing essays, others go to pieces in an oral. And finally, the method of marking: is the marker consistent? Does he, if several people are involved, keep to the same standard as the rest? Is the marking accurate? Or has someone, somewhere, added up wrong?

I hope that no one would conclude from this that, if educational measurement is as shaky as that, it is not worth bothering about. The reasons why we need to make assessments still hold good. The moral rather is that we should try to make our assessments as reliable as possible (having first done our best to ensure validity), and even then, regard any single assessment of a child with a fair bit of suspicion. It is no more than a spot check. Coupled with others, it may indicate a trend, and then it should be taken heed of, but on its own we should not attach too much importance to it.

Public examinations are, of course, spot checks too and the same applies to them. It is not a happy situation that many people in this country attach far too much importance to examination results, using them for selection purposes for which they were not intended, and attributing to the examiners quite superhuman powers of divination. Unfortunately, you can never win. If you go for continuous assessment, rather than an examination, so as to even out the pupils' variability, you have a much greater problem in maintaining the markers' consistency of standards over the period.

Comparability

This brings us to the third aspect that we ought to look at: comparability. Perhaps comparability is rather neglected in the literature, in comparison with the other two aspects, but it covers some very live issues. Is it easier to get a CSE grade 1 or an O level A–C? Is it easier to get an O level in the winter or the summer? Is Mode III easier than Mode I?

Within the school, too, comparability is one of the key issues in matters of subject choice, reporting to parents and monitoring progress, as already touched upon. Unless we can be sure that any given grade represents our best attempt at assessment in that subject, rather than being an expression of the grader's personal whim, the information we collect and give out is of dubious value – perhaps of no value at all, in extreme cases.

People sometimes reveal strangely emotional attitudes when these questions are raised. Marking seems to be an intensely personal procedure and any suggestion that marks might be scaled or adjusted in some way is somehow interpreted as an attack on personal or professional integrity. 'I gave him 52 per cent and nobody's going to muck *my* marks around.'

I taught in a school once which followed the dubious practice of streaming on the aggregate of marks in all subjects. As is the nature of things, of course, teachers in the English department tended to bunch their marks together, between 70 per cent and 30 per cent, usually, while the mathematicians, as is their wont, happily filled the whole scale from 0 to 100 per cent. Now, there is a well-known statistical phenomenon about combining marks: the final rank order is much more heavily influenced by marks which are spread out than by those which are bunched together and, in extreme cases, the bunched marks may have no effect on the final order, which is wholly determined by the well-spread marks. Which explains why the mathematics department were quite happy with our streaming policy, but the English teachers kept wondering vaguely how their best students were ending up in the bottom stream.

This is one of the arguments to raise with those who object to any standardizing of marks: if this is not done, children may be unfairly penalized, purely as a result of statistical side-effects. These side-effects may, of course, occur within a department when, for example, you try to add course-work marks (which tend to bunch) to examination marks which may be more spread out. The other relevant issues of inter-pretation of marks or grades by parents, etc., has already been touched on.

These are important questions which really should be the subject of school policy decisions and, as head of department, it is your responsibility to ensure that they are carried out as far as your subject is concerned. These matters are certainly proper topics for heads of department meetings and also for discussion and implementation within your area of responsi-bility. I guarantee that you can stir the sleepiest department into life by a discussion of marks and marking!

The base for the assessment

We ought to turn now to look at the questions which you will have to decide with your colleagues when planning an assessment programme within your department. First of all, we can distinguish four main test types:

1 *Mastery tests or criterion-referenced tests*
   These measure 'mastery' of a defined battery of skills — the criterion. The commonest example is the driving test where the examiners have a certain body of skills in mind (reversing round a corner, the three-point turn, etc.) which you must have mastered before you can be let out on the road on your own. The different 'standards' in music are another example. Modern language teachers in various parts of the country are investigating the possibility of this type of test for their subject. The mastery test is essentially a pass/fail test; either you have reached the criterion, or not.

2 *Discriminating tests or norm-referenced tests*
   These aim to distinguish different levels of attainment as clearly as possible and usually do so with reference to the group — the norm. Most public examinations are basically norm-referenced (the CSE grade 4 is the standard for an average 16-year-old) as are most school tests and examin-ations (the norm being the class- or the year-group).

3 *Diagnostic tests*
   Where these are intended to discover the cause of some fundamental learning disability, they will probably be used by a psychologist in a one-to-one situation. Diagnostic

information for the teacher can be obtained from almost any test, if he looks, and we shall come back to that later.

4 *Predictive or aptitude tests*

The most familiar example is the 11+ and we know what became of that! Aptitude tests are used widely in personnel selection but they are rather dubious. Predictive validity of some commonly accepted measures is very small; A-level grades, as a predictor of final degree level, for example, have been shown to be not much better than using a pin.

I would like now to try to pull some of these strands together and to consider the practical implications. There are five key areas that we ought to look at. First, the issue of measurement (can we actually make the assessment?). Then, we want to know if the assessments will give us information on progress. At some stage, we shall need to be able to relate to external standards. We shall probably want to know how the individual child being assessed stands in relation to other children. And we shall want to know how the assessment in one subject compares with another. If we consider these five areas in relation to four possible assessment bases — assessment in relation to the child's potential; in relation to the class or set; in relation to the year-group; and in relation to an objective criterion — we can see the drawbacks of each as shown in the table on page 82.

My own preference has probably become clear: in comparison with the many difficulties associated with other methods, norm-referenced assessment in relation to the year-group is a comparatively stable measure. It has one serious weakness: since each year-group is its own base, norm-referencing cannot show any progress (or decline!) in standards of teaching. Samples of work can be kept from year to year for subjective comparison; samples should be taken from the full range of ability and, as far as possible, represent the whole range of work covered.

Perhaps I should add a few words here about assessment in relation to potential, which has done rather badly in the table, but which is sometimes advocated by those who dislike the 'competitive' element in norm-referenced tests. Assuming for the moment that there is an acceptable measure of potential, assessment in relation to this base will mean that a child who fulfils his potential will be graded A. This will be so whether his potential is that of a first-class honours graduate or of barely mastering the basic skills of literacy by the end of the fifth year. No information on the relative standards between these two is given. Both have received A and, from the experience of schools which have tried this method, it is virtually

Table 6.1 Bases for the assessment

Assessment of the child in relation to:	Measurement	Progress	External standards	Other children	Other subjects
Objective criterion	✓ (once the criterion is identified)	✗ (unless there is a succession of criteria)	✗ (not used in external exams)	? (limited to yes/no with regard to one criterion)	✗ (criteria in each almost certainly not comparable)
Class or set	✓ (no unusual problems)	✓ (straightforward)	✓(?) (but may depend on accuracy of setting)	✓ (in set or class, but ? in year-group)	✓(?) (depends on method of setting)
Year-group	✓ (straightforward except for non-readers)	✓	✓ (no unusual problems)	✓	✓(?) (may be some problems with half-groups in practical subjects)
Child's potential	✗ (is there any reliable method of gauging potential?)	✗ (unless there is a base in column 1)	✗ (no information)	✗ (no information except in so far as each realizes own potential)	✗ (potential in each would have to be established)

impossible to explain to parents why the two children should not have an equal chance of a university place. Even if it is explained, parents could rightly complain that the school was giving them inadequate information, by not relating their child's attainments to external standards.

Analysis of test results

At this stage, people sometimes begin to get a little wary and to think that a lot of heavy mathematics is involved. You *can* go in for factor analysis and similar esoterica, if you enjoy that sort of thing, but it is not essential. The most important step is the planning of the test, as I have already discussed. When you have finished drafting your test or examination paper, give it to someone else to read and comment on. Work out model answers too, so that your colleague can see what you expect. By the time you get the paper back, in addition to your colleague's amendments, I am fairly sure you will see half a dozen things that you will wish to alter. Time is of the essence: give yourself time to plan, time to draft and redraft.

When you have finished your marking, do you just throw the papers away? You are losing valuable information if you do. Check on the working of your test. If you are trying to discriminate, have you succeeded? Draw a histogram of the marks; are they spread out, or bunched in the middle? If they are bunched, it means you are wasting your mark range, which means poor discrimination and a waste of examining time. Was the marking consistent? Try a re-mark exercise after a month or so and see.

Look at the test again. What did they get wrong? Even a simple list of wrong answers can often give invaluable diagnostic information. Were there any questions that everyone got right? These contribute nothing to the effectiveness of the test, though you may still wish to retain them — easy 'starters', for example, or an internal mastery test on certain key concepts which you expect every child to have learned.

You can go a little further without much difficulty, if you wish. There are techniques available which require no more mathematical skill than counting, adding up and making a percentage. These operations are enormously simplified by the purchase of a small electronic calculator, such as you can buy for a few pounds.

This sort of analysis is useful, certainly, but by no means essential. The main thing is to be absolutely clear in your thinking about what you are trying to do and not to take things for granted. 'Of course, old Bill and I mark the same way — known him for years.' Well . . . maybe . . . or maybe not. Do not assume it — find out.

PART THREE

The Subject and the Skills

The process of drawing up, ensuring adherence to, and reviewing a scheme of work is obviously a major concern of the head of every department in every school. These final chapters argue that any statement of content, aims and objectives must encourage both teachers and pupils to understand and use vital skills that enable effective learning to take place.

7 Drawing up a scheme of work
Michael Marland

The need

In the British school the main burden of curriculum planning is placed on the heads of departments, and their task is expressed in the department's 'syllabus'. Teachers have been used to being handed a 'syllabus' by their head of department, and throughout the careers of most teachers the term 'syllabus' has had unfortunate connotations: it is presumed to be 'cramping', 'over-full', or 'rigid'. Many of us have thus come to regard the syllabus as something to be fought — like examinations, headteachers, and caretakers. We can really teach, we feel, only when we are free of it.

Understandable as that emotion may be from time to time, if each of us is to work as part of a team, both within the department and across the school as a whole, and if education is to be more than the chance results of the additive process described in Chapter 1 by Maurice Holt, there has to be a plan, and that is bound to be embodied in some form of syllabus or scheme of work.[1] In many ways I prefer the common American phrase 'curriculum guidelines', for it allows something both wider ('curriculum' rather than 'syllabus') and freer ('guidelines'). Whatever the word used, there is a need for a 'book of the department'.

Oddly, 'curriculum' is also a word that rather frightens many teachers. (I have even heard it said by a junior school head that 'There's nothing in curriculum for younger or less able pupils'!) As the concept of curriculum that is most useful for the basis of departmental thinking I suggest Lawrence Stenhouse's definition: 'A curriculum is an attempt to communicate the essential principles and features of an educational proposal in such a form that it is open to critical

[1] The Bullock Report came to use the awkward phrase 'instruments of policy', largely out of an attempt (misguided in my view) to avoid the associations of the alternative phrases.

scrutiny and capable of effective translation into practice.'[1]

Each of the elements in that definition is important for the head of department:

1 There has to be 'an educational proposal'. We have to propose what is to be achieved; even the most apparently informal activity with young people has an ambition — even a walk in the park. In professional terms that ambition has to be articulated in the form of a proposal.
2 There has to be 'an attempt to communicate'; a curriculum cannot be secret. The proposal has to be capable of communication to pupils, to parents, to other colleagues, to governors, to yourself and your team.
3 There has to be a possibility of 'effective translation into practice': this means that the educational proposal must be defined in a way that it can be carried out. As I shall argue later, many syllabuses start with aims ludicrously unreal or vague.

So far I have spoken of the 'scheme of work' as if it were the physical book. However, it is the thinking embodied in the document that is really the centre of our concern. Indeed it might be argued that the prime aim of the scheme of work is to demonstrate *to yourself* the process of thinking that lies within the planning. I cannot accept that a properly developed and properly interrelated curriculum plan can be held independently in a variety of people's heads. It must have a documentary form, but it must be realized that the document is only the physical embodiment of the process, and that process and its results are the real 'scheme'.

There is considerable evidence from the reports of careful observation of schools that the quality of schemes of work is inadequate in our schools. In 1977, for instance, a report by HM Inspectorate was published on work in modern languages in eighty-three schools, and it complained that a very large number of departments visited had no scheme of work or syllabus.[2] This is echoed in an Inner London Education Authority report, which says: 'It is surprising that even among heads of departments there is disagreement as to what it [a scheme of work] should contain.'[3] In 1973 and 1974 I was one of those who visited schools for the Bullock Committee. We were amazed to find that the majority of departments

[1] Lawrence Stenhouse, *An Introduction to Curriculum Research and Development* (Heinemann Educational Books, 1975), p. 4.

[2] Department of Education and Science, *Modern Languages in Comprehensive Schools* (HMSO, 1977).

[3] Inner London Education Authority, *Modern Languages in Comprehensive Schools* (ILEA, 1978).

did not have an adequate or active syllabus. Indeed many had none at all. Similar criticisms were voiced by HMIs in describing primary schools in their 1979 report:

> In a quarter of the schools in the survey teachers with positions of curricular or organisational responsibility were having a noticeable influence on the quality of work in the school as a whole. In the remaining schools there was little evidence that the influence of teachers with curricular responsibilities spread beyond the work in their own classes . . . 85 per cent or more of the schools had schemes of work in mathematics and English. Nearly three-quarters of the schools had written guidelines for religious education . . . In any other subject fewer than half the schools had a scheme of work. There was evidence in the survey that where a teacher with a special responsibility was able to exercise it through the planning and supervision of a programme of work, this was effective in raising the standards of work and the levels of expectation of what children were capable of doing.[1]

The actual percentage of primary schools without any guidelines or schemes of work for each aspect of the curriculum are shocking: for example, language, 15 per cent; science, 57 per cent; history, 64 per cent; social studies, 82 per cent.[2] We do not have strictly comparable observations for secondary schools, for the HMI survey[3] was organized differently and written up in a different form. However, reading carefully the diplomatically put observations, a similarly worrying picture of failure in syllabus and scheme-of-work planning can be noticed:

> The planning of coherent policies and their effective implementation require the collective involvement of the whole staff. They also require clear and effective leadership, by heads and by heads of department and senior staff. The indications are that collective thinking and planning are difficult to achieve, even where there is an appreciation of the need . . . The discussion of policies, their translation into the planning of specific programmes of work in the classroom, their regular assessment and evaluation take more time than many teachers have available to them.[4]

Perhaps the deficiency is most compellingly, if reticently, put in the research published under the title *How Teachers Plan Their Courses*: 'There is little consistency in the role which the syllabus plays, and some doubt must be entertained about whether teachers consider that the syllabus is serving any worthwhile purpose at all'.[5] Corroborative evidence will

---

[1] Department of Education and Science, *Primary Education in England* (HMSO, 1978), p. 37.
[2] ibid., derived from Table 25 (p. 40).
[3] Department of Education and Science, *Aspects of Secondary Education in England* (HMSO, 1979).
[4] pp. 263–4.
[5] Philip H. Taylor, *How Teachers Plan Their Courses* (Windsor: NFER Publishing, 1978), p. 51.

be found in the analysis of the use of secondary teachers'
time. Hilsum and Strong found time spent on an immense
variety of activities, but little attendance at professional
meetings and little time spent on the curriculum and syllabus.[1]

Thus it can be fairly said that, despite the emphasis the
country puts on school-based curriculum planning, and
despite the hard work of many teachers, there is a worrying
gap in the actual curriculum planning done within most
schools, and this manifests itself both at whole-school planning levels and at departmental syllabus planning level.
This is in many ways not surprising. We arc all catapulted
into, or we fight our way into, our head of department posts
without any real training in curriculum planning, indeed
most of the literature on curriculum planning bears very
little relationship to the nature of the task which is actually
required by schools.[2] It is interesting to note that the Schools
Council's current proposals for its future work put a great
emphasis on helping school-based curriculum planning. But
we have not had much help so far.

To make things worse, there is the fallacy that 'textbook
subjects' do not need a scheme of work. So that modern
languages, science and mathematics departments, for instance,
often feel that because they have bought in a textbook, they
have removed the need for a scheme of work. Certainly such
a department's 'book of the department' would take a different form, one in which perhaps the course book or the
printed material would be an integral part, or possibly an
appendix, but that does not alter the need for devising a
proper scheme of work around it in the school.

There are other fallacies as well. There is a theory that
small departments do not require such aids: 'After all, there
are only two teachers in the music department, and one or
two people who come in part time; they are *always* talking
to each other . . .' This, I think, is even worse, because in the
very small department it is possible to go on having these
kind of informal half-conversations, which are very valuable
but not sufficient for drawing up a proper programme of
work. Indeed, such conversations can mask the real need.
There is another theory that stable departments do not
require a scheme of work: 'We've mostly been here for years,

---

[1] S. Hilsum and C. Strong, *The Secondary Teacher's Day* (Windsor: NFER
Publishing, 1978), for example, page 153.
[2] An exception to this is Alan Blyth et al., *Place, Time and Society 8—13:
Curriculum Planning in History, Geography and Social Science* published by
Collins/ESL Bristol for the Schools Council (1976). This works from the basic
thesis that curriculum planning is done by teams of teachers in schools, and gives
some guidance on how it might be done.

and everyone knows what they're doing.' Possibly members
of such a departmental team have the greatest need for a
proper scheme. Finally, there is the misguidedly elevated
fallacy that some subjects are too subtle, serious, intangible,
or important to be described in the form of a syllabus. Thus
one music adviser declared: 'All that can usefully be said
about the teaching of music can be written on the back of a
matchbox.' Similarly, teachers of art, drama, and English
have been known to instance the sheer importance of their
subject as being beyond any syllabus. One cannot help having
some sympathy with this point of view; indeed there is some
faint truth in it. However, the fact that the ultimate heights
of an activity cannot easily be defined is no excuse for not
planning a course and for not going as far as is possible in
describing the educational proposal. As Hilda Taba comments:
'The often referred to intangibility of some objectives is
nothing but a smokescreen for lack of clarity.'[1]

I want to portray the scheme of work not as a cramping
set of instructions, but essentially as something enabling —
enabling the individual teacher to work more profitably
by what it offers him. I do not consider that the apparent
freedom you get from having no such scheme is true freedom:
it is mere impotence. Without a curriculum, you cannot
build on what others have done; you cannot expect others
to build on what you have done; there can be no relationship between the work of an individual and the school
as a whole; there can be no true continuity. Of course,
there is going to have to be constant revision of a scheme
of work, but without such a properly planned curriculum
you cannot fulfil your true purposes or aims — or even truly
have any!

Purpose and audience

One unhappy result of the denigration of the schemes of
work is that many teachers have lost sight of the uses of the
document itself, coming to see it as a prestige piece of 'wall-
papering', as the cynical saying goes, for visiting inspectors.
I intend to start, therefore, by sorting out the various purposes of the document itself, and the audience envisaged for
each of these purposes: what is it for?; whom is it for?

There are five main purposes for a departmental curriculum
document:

---

[1] Hilda Taba, *Curriculum Development: Theory and Practice* (New York:
Harcourt Brace Jovanovich, 1962), p. 199.

1 *Analysis and planning.* To help the team with their thinking and decision-making, and it is not just the end-product of that process. Its assistance to analysis for the team itself is undoubtedly the most important purpose.
2 *Internal co-operation.* To facilitate co-operation between the teachers of that team.
3 *Whole-school co-operation.* To make it possible for the work of an individual team of teachers to carry out the overall aims of the school, and to facilitate co-operation across the whole school and between teams of teachers.
4 *Induction.* To facilitate the induction of student teachers, probationers and other more experienced new teachers.
5 *Publicity.* To provide a manifesto for others who need to know of the work of the department.

Each of these five different, though closely related, purposes has a different *audience*:

1 *The head of department and the team drawing up the scheme.* The planning and drafting provides a focusing and reflecting back of the thinking, and the first audience is therefore those responsible for the planning.
2 *The departmental team.* These must read it for their departmental co-operation.
3 *Senior staff, other heads of department, and pastoral heads.* They must be familiar with it so that they can appropriately influence later developments, can respond in their own planning and teaching, and can counsel pupils suitably. (There are a very large number of heads of department who look a bit puzzled if you say, 'Could your scheme of work be available for the heads of year?'. They look at you as if you had suggested that the scheme of work might be of interest to the caretaker or the man who runs the local fish-and-chip shop. Yet it is the pastoral team who are giving educational, vocational and personal guidance to the pupils. They should actually be party to the drawing up of the syllabuses, and they must know what is going on. They can hardly be expected to advise pupils adequately if they do not know what it is they are advising them into. In my view many of the criticisms of option systems in schools are really criticisms of the relationship between academic planning and pastoral guidance.)
4 *Students and new teachers.* These need a rapid way of finding what it is they are fitting in to and are going to contribute to.
5 *Inspectors and advisers, governors, parents' committee, and any other interested 'outsiders'.* All these have the right to easy access to a description of what is intended.

The purposes and audiences of the document can be laid out thus:

Purpose	Audience
1 Thinking	Departmental team
2 Internal co-operation	Departmental team
3 Whole-school co-operation	All teachers
4 Induction	Students and new teachers
5 Publicity	Advisers, governors, parents, etc.

If some such breakdown of the purposes and intended audiences of the final document is accepted, it is possible to go back to the beginning and ask about the content of a scheme of work. This involves a consideration of curriculum planning — not just at the syllabus planning level, but at the whole-school level.

Curriculum planning

The planning of a departmental scheme of work is only part of the process of school-based curriculum planning, and before considering the departmental task I need to suggest ways in which the ideal school should set about its overall curriculum planning. None of us works in an ideal school, but we constantly have to try to cope with day-to-day needs by current methods, while adjusting our medium- and long-term planning to rather better methods. I want to suggest that most curriculum planning in schools gets the cart before the horse. It goes something like this. We have a group of teachers called a history department; what should 'history' teach? In that case, the cart is the history department and the horse is what should be taught. I believe the question should be the other way round. The confusion comes from defining and creating a team (the history department) with an implied purpose (teaching history) before defining what the pupils should learn and the school should teach. It has been seen (though why is not clear) as 'progressive' to put the questions slightly differently, but still in the fundamentally wrong order. 'We have a history department, but as it's not right to plan in units, with what other team can we join them?' In other words to 'integrate'. This is equally objectionable, as it is a planning process that does not start from the 'educational proposal' of what should be learnt, but from the existence of a department or a subject. Indeed the very word 'integrate' embodies a curriculum fallacy, as it paradoxically presumes the existence of separate teaching entities before a consideration of what should be taught. (The better process may still produce a team with responsibilities larger than 'history', but the process is from *division* of teaching aims, not 'integration' of aims.) There are three steps to curriculum planning, and they do not start with the team of historians or the team of scientists, but with what the school considers pupils need to know.

1 *Listing content*

The first step is simply drawing up 'a shopping list', if you like -- a list of what it is that would go into the school's educational proposal. Obviously that is a large task, but it is actually much easier than to start at the other end and ask 'What's in the shopping basket at the moment? And what are we going to throw out?' It is both easier and more logical to go back to the beginning. No doubt it will be necessary to have some way of focusing the search for what is to be listed on the basic curriculum plan. However, it is best to find as modes of focusing labels which are not those of subject (or pastoral) teams; otherwise the nature of the activity is virtually automatically fixed by the choice of team (for example, library-user education looks different if its components are listed with general application to a school than it does if they are listed after a preliminary decision that it is a matter for the English department). Such likely focuses are the 'personal curriculum', aspects of society such as 'technology', 'work'; skills such as 'language', 'study skills and reading', 'visual literacy', 'numeracy'.

2 *Distribution*

The next task is to distribute the listed items to teams of teachers. There are three main ways of distributing any part of the curriculum shopping list. These can be most easily understood if you take as an example a facet of the curriculum such as some aspects of preparation for work and further and higher education. If that has been identified as being on the basic curriculum check-list or outline proposals for the school, it has to be decided who is to be responsible for teaching it. The three distribution methods are:

(a) *Single team*

The easiest (and the one that heads like best) is to have a team of teachers (called perhaps 'Careers' in this case) and give them the responsibility for this facet of the curriculum. The matter can then be ticked off because you know you have got a head of careers, who will be teaching those skills and those concepts. I call that the 'single team' method. It is the most common and the most convenient from the head's point of view, and is part of the main historical tradition that Maurice Holt outlined in Chapter 1. For instance, library-user education and study skills could, under this first method, be given completely to one particular team, the English teachers.[1] You could even invent a team called the 'Department of Study Skills', and leave it to them, just like some schools have a team called 'Personal Responsibility Department' for guidance.

(b) Multi-team

The second method of distribution is to say that as the school is organized at the moment there is not a single team which can cover this package or bundle of items. It can therefore be decided to distribute this facet of the curriculum *between different teams.* You might take health education and decide to give part of the package to the science department, part to the home economics department, and part to the tutorial staff. That is neither 'integration' nor mere 'co-operation'; it is taking a coherent body of items from the original shopping list, and dividing them out between teams. Thus it can be called a multi-team approach. For instance, library-user education and study skills would not be allocated to 'English' alone, but some items would go to the tutorial team (after all you can hardly have personal and educational guidance given by people who do not take any interest in study skills, learning skills, and the use of the library), another part to the humanities team, and another part to the science team. This method is a little more difficult for headteachers, because of the problems of co-ordination. Who is going to co-ordinate these things which are in different teams? Sadly in too many schools the director of studies is too busy doing cover slips to achieve this co-ordination!

(c) Whole-school

The third method of distribution is that of whole-school policies, in which the syllabus within every departmental team includes a part of the curriculum facet under consideration. This last is possibly the most powerful. But it is also immensely difficult. So much so that Maurice Holt called it (Chapter 1) 'the weak scheme'. Although he did not mean weak to be perjorative, clearly one of the reasons for

---

[1] See the report of the British Library/Schools Council seminar on information skills held in January 1980 (Methuen Educational, 1980).

calling it weak is because it is very difficult to exert power to make it happen effectively. The possibility is that if everyone is supposed to be a teacher of careers, nobody will actually be a teacher of careers. Most commonly, schools endeavour to have language policies as 'whole-school' distribution. There are many other curriculum facets that could be thus treated: for example, technology, health, careers.[1]

The pros and cons of each of those distributive methods are clear: the first risks decontexturalized isolation, but has the advantage of ensuring that a group of teachers cover the topic thoroughly, and that every pupil can meet this team. The last has the advantage of relevance and interrelatedness, but has the disadvantage that if you are not careful little is actually taught, and the whole-school policy is not implemented.

3 Syllabus planning

Only at this stage, after the whole-school lists have been drawn up and distributed between teams, is it really possible to make a start on the scheme of work for the individual team. To start earlier is to risk omission between subject teams (a common problem, as illustrated by, for example, pupils' ignorance of town planning and architecture, careers, or large parts of the world, such as Islam) or confusing overlaps. It certainly is to risk the loss of mutual support and reinforcement (for example, by teaching approaches to graphs that are common across the curriculum).

The school in which you are working as head of department is unlikely to have attempted such a methodical approach to the basis of the curriculum, but there may well be sympathy from other head of department colleagues for an attempt to be made to start on at least some 'across the curriculum' plans. Certainly it is extraordinarily difficult to plan the contents of one departmental curriculum until these broader approaches are also planned. Even if there are no such whole-school policies and, for the moment at least, you do not see any way of influencing the rest of the school to produce them, it is important to bear in mind the first two stages of curriculum planning before you come to the third. It is almost as if you should, at least in outline, go through those two stages for yourself as a way of clarifying your

[1] For a fuller discussion see Michael Marland, 'The pastoral curriculum', in Ron Best, et al., *Perspectives on Pastoral Care* (Heinemann Educational Books, 1980), and Michael Marland, *The Comprehensive Curriculum* (Heinemann Educational Books, forthcoming).

approach to the curriculum planning of your own team. The next section, therefore, considers in detail that third stage of curriculum planning — the scheme of work within the department.

Influences on the scheme of work

How should a teacher team, led by its head of department, decide what is to go into the team's scheme of work? What are the influences that the head of department should search out and react to in leading the discussion? There are a number, and their relative importance will vary from time to time and from school to school. The head of department must ensure that all the influences are appropriately felt, and not over-react to just one. It is too easy and too common for a departmental team to work from a narrow range of influence.

1 *Pupils*

Although it may seem obvious that the needs of the pupils come first, I hesitate in so placing this influence lest a new social and intellectual determinism should creep in. Both the extreme right and the extreme left can slip into a deterministic approach of accepting the present situation of the pupil as defining the most important influence on the curriculum. Such an attitude can sound all right, but may limit the pupil's range of possibilities, with no strong attempt to raise their aspirations.

2 *Whole-school policies*

Logically, whole-school policies should precede more narrow 'subject' policies: thus the detailed working out of a history syllabus should be within a wider humanities syllabus, and that should be planned after the school has drawn up its personal curriculum, study-skills curriculum, and so forth. One of the reasons why in the years after the Bullock report 'language across the curriculum' proved so difficult to establish in a school was because it was a *broader* policy which schools were endeavouring to devise over and round smaller, unrelated policies.

3 *The subject*

The arguments about the existence or otherwise of 'subjects' have been confused by the pro- and anti-integration debates.

There is no need to see a polarized debate here: a pupil's learning needs and many facets of education are hierarchically wider than subjects, but subjects can and do have their own cohesion. Many apparently experienced heads of departments nevertheless seem to find it difficult to focus on the particular contribution of their own subject, quoting as its especial justification aims which are equally those of a number of other traditional teaching subjects. When asked what is the particular contribution to the curriculum of their subject, I have heard head after head of department give the same sort of answer, such as 'It helps pupils understand their environment'. (In trying to argue for the centrality of their subject, they are in fact arguing for the possibility of disposing of it!) Thus, 'deduction from evidence' is a curriculum aim that should be on a whole-school curriculum policy, and relates to many activities – science; craft, design, and technology; history; English literature; etc. However, there is still a need to understand and respond to the nature of each subject, in particular its own hierarchy of logic, its own style of questioning, and its own body of facts.

4 *Public examinations*

Contrary to what is often said, the UK system of external public examinations is best seen as a way of reinforcing the curriculum autonomy of the school: alternative methods of monitoring the work of pupils and teachers involve week-by-week external control, whereas the examination system considers only the end-product. Thus the school, and within it each department, is free to develop its work as it considers best, provided only that the pupils can as a whole reasonably meet the criteria of the school-selected examination at the end. Thus 16-plus examinations can be thought of as a protective umbrella for internal curriculum planning. Despite this, many heads of departments regrettably see the external examination board as having fixed the school's subject syllabus, and there is therefore no further need for considering it.

In the first place, there is, of course, a choice of examinations. Even given the administrative difficulties of a school's using too many boards, there is the choice of CSE or O-level; in the former a choice of Modes; in the latter, of boards; in both cases, of examination subject; then often there is a choice of paper; and finally, of sections within the paper. Further, an examination syllabus is not a teaching syllabus. An outline of what method of testing will be used on which aspects of content does not adequately detail the teaching approach for the years preparing for the examination, still less for the younger years. Indeed examiners' reports over long periods of time have, rightly, complained that candidates have lacked, for instance, the power to interpret data, or have submitted projects with little sign of personal organization of the material. This kind of criticism I take to be a criticism of the school's subject syllabus: the department have taken it that the board's syllabus has settled all.

5 Schemes from elsewhere

A very useful step is to gather fairly widely other syllabuses and subject schemes. These will include not only the syllabuses of departments whose tasks are broadly similar to yours in other schools, but also published schemes. Published schemes include those, usually comprehensive ones, devised by research and development teams under the auspices of publicly funded bodies, such as the Schools Council and the Nuffield Foundation. There is also the range of textbooks from educational publishers, many of which are in effect schemes of work. Inspection copies can be borrowed, and the easiest and most thorough way is to circulate the publishers and specify what you are searching for. (As mentioned in Chapter 4, a list of educational publishers can be obtained from the Educational Publishers Council.) Finally, the various subject associations often publish schemes of work for aspects of their subject, sometimes as supplements to their magazines or as articles in them. Some of them have small libraries and information offices willing to help.

Having gathered this hoard of other people's ideas, a methodical culling of valuable organizing principles and ideas needs to be carried out. This is not a job for one person, but the material should be distributed with an agreed analytic approach to each member of the team. Their findings will then be pooled — not as a way of selecting 'the best', but to illuminate the department's own planning process.

6 Other subjects

Some other departmental teams are obviously concerned with work especially close to yours. Ideally, the departmental planning team should study, at least briefly, the schemes of work of every other team (including the pastoral programme used by the tutors, if there is one!), and discuss how the work will relate to them. In practice this may be over-ambitious, but certainly the cognate subjects should be studied very carefully, particularly those with some emphasis on similar skills: for instance, scientists should study the schemes in technology, mathematics, home economics, health education, library and study skills.

7 *The teachers*

It is always a delicate balance to decide how much the work of a school should be related to the particular strengths and enthusiasms of the existing teachers. The advantages are: more expertise, more enthusiasm; the disadvantages are that the work can become self-indulgent, with more pleasure for the teacher than significance for the learner; the approach can become unbalanced, with important aspects of the subject under-stressed; and when teachers leave, continuity is extra difficult. We all have weaker sides to our teaching, and too much dependence on the existing strengths of a group of teachers tends to allow the weak aspects to weaken further, until they atrophy and virtually disappear. Conversely, some teachers over-play their own strengths — the book they know well, the laboratory approach, the workshop exercise — until they virtually parody themselves. Probably it would be unwise to embark on a media course, a study of plastics, or the Caribbean without the expertise, but it is a dangerous tendency to look too narrowly at existing expertise and enthusiasm. Clearly a balance is required: a team would be well advised to assess its strengths in relation to its teaching ambitions and, although the syllabus can reasonably be devised out of the team's characteristics, it may be necessary to adjust those characteristics (by in-service work, or by especial care over the next appointment) rather than to adjust the scheme of work. Indeed the process of planning a scheme of work is also a self-assessment exercise for the teaching team.

Objectives

After considering the influences on the scheme of work, the first step in drafting must be to establish the objectives for the team in such a way that they are consistent with, and develop within, the whole-school objectives.

Schools, and departmental teams within schools, do not seem to be too keen on defining objectives. I think that this may be because if we are not careful the objectives are drafted in a way that is objectionably highfaluting and grandiose. From this, perhaps, comes the school-teacherly fear that objectives are not practical. In fact, of course, there is a vitally practical function for objectives: without a specification of the objectives of an educational activity, it is not possible to proceed with any detailed planning, for the objectives for a course actually help with both the content and the method. Given the incredible range of possible topics, how can you decide what to put in, for instance, a science course or a humanities course, without a set of objectives to use as criteria?

Curiously, many in education see objectives as being of little importance for the less able and below average. It is as if teachers are saying that with these pupils any hope of learning is so slight it is pointless having any objectives. Work from hand-to-mouth, and anything they learn is an unexpected bonus. When so little is expected, why define objectives, for anything is better than nothing? On the contrary, with less-able pupils objectives are particularly important. After all, by definition, these are pupils who will understand somewhat less, remember somewhat less, and go less far in education. What is included in their courses, therefore, has to be rigorously selected, and the criteria for inclusion in a syllabus equally so.

Indeed, everything in a syllabus must earn its keep, for there is no time to include anything that cannot be strictly justified. Perhaps the best remark on the key principal in curriculum planning comes not from the weightier tomes but from Jerome K. Jerome's *Three Men In a Boat*. In it one of the characters declares, as they are packing: 'It's not what you can do with, but what you can't do without that matters.' The same is true of syllabus planning: nothing should be included if it can be done without. It is to objectives that the departmental team must look for criteria by which to judge the inclusion or otherwise of an item. Therefore the objectives need careful consideration, and re-consideration, not only at all the planning stages, but also through the operational life of the syllabus. The art of curriculum building includes *discarding*, and the set of objective definitions is the *discarding mesh*. However, this emphasis on the necessity for objectives is not only justified by the question of topic selection. The methodology and pupil activity, the focus of the topics, and the whole style of the approach to the topic or activity will come out of the definition of the objectives.

It is not at all easy to draw up objectives, and many that grace departmental syllabuses are useless, in the strict sense that, however euphonious, they cannot be *used* in later elaboration of the syllabus or its implementation. There seem to be three main types of fault in syllabus objectives:

1 *The hopelessly vague*

Many syllabus objectives include sentences which sound good when you start reading them, but which on closer scrutiny actually say very little: 'The aim of history (or science, or English, et al.) is to prepare young people for their place in the modern world'. Yes, that is an unexceptional sentiment, but it is too vague to stand as an objective, at least without closer analysis and breaking down into more specific objectives. We cannot leave objectives as vague as: 'To develop in the pupils minds that can cope with the complexities of modern life'; or 'To encourage a knowledge and attitude necessary for being a responsible citizen'; although both could be used as a starting-point for more precise objectives. As they stand, these are the kind of objective that is axiomatic, and could belong equally to any set of objectives for any educational activity.

2 *The grandiose*

This category often merges with the first, as it is aiming for the impressive that often leads to vagueness. This characteristic has been observed in the USA by Hilda Taba, who tartly records: 'Units with elaborate objectives decorating their front pages, and with no signs of experiences planned to make them an actuality, are legion.'[1]

A clue to the grandiose is the use of impenetrable and hopeless jargon. There can be a real function for jargon – to frame or highlight comparatively ordinary events so that we look at them afresh from a particular point of view. Not all jargon, therefore, is either useless or harmful. Nevertheless, some jargon merely obscures, making it seem as if something of significance is being said when there is no real content. This seems a particular temptation in writing educational objectives. The following example may be an unusually exaggerated one, but can we not recognize the schoolteacher's temptation to describe what we are aiming at in complex jargon really because we are not too sure? The father of a secondary-school pupil in Texas received the following curriculum description from the school:

> Our school's Cross-Graded, Multi-Ethnic, Individualised Learning Programme is designed to enhance the concept of an open-ended Learning Programme with emphasis on a continuum of multi-ethnic academically enriched learning, using the identified intellectually gifted child as the agent or director of his own learning. Major emphasis is on cross-graded, multi-ethnic learning with the main objective being to learn respect for the uniqueness of the person.

[1] Hilda Taba, *Curriculum Development*, op. cit., p. 204.

If that was the version of the curriculum objectives sent home to parents, one wonders what the version prepared for professionals was like. It is reported that the father wrote back:

> I have a degree, speak two foreign languages and four Indian dialects, and make my living as a wordsmith, but I haven't the faintest idea what the hell you are talking about. Have you?

3 The discrepant

I mean by this, the statement which is acceptable in itself, but has no functional relationship with the syllabus that follows. I can think for instance of a third-year history syllabus which included among its five objectives: (a) to give a sense of chronology; and (b) to help the pupils interpret evidence. However, in the first place the syllabus was organized around a number of themes from the twentieth century, with no sign of how this would help the pupil gather a sense of historical progression and chronology; secondly, there was no content in the syllabus which actually gave the opportunity to interpret evidence and no mention of tuition in the skills required. In another history syllabus I read the following objective: 'To develop the ability to extract relevant facts from various sources of information, e.g. written material, pictorial material, statistics, and maps'. I was disappointed then to find throughout the remainder of the syllabus no later reference to:

(a) The skills that would have to be taught to achieve this
(b) Materials recommended for use that would be suitable for this emphasis
(c) Any ways in which to integrate these skills with the topics suggested
(d) How to focus the syllabus from this point of view.

Objectives can be described at various levels of generality, from the broadest (that is, highest levels of generality) to the narrow and specific (that is, lower levels of generality). Indeed some people keep the word 'aims' for the most general — for example, 'To develop critical awareness'. Such people would keep the word 'objectives' for more specific statements of observable behaviour — for example, 'When given a description of a research design problem, the student can select correctly from the x statistical procedures covered.' For the purposes of my discussion of the departmental scheme of work, I shall blur the distinction, calling all descriptions of what we are hoping to achieve in the students as a result of the teaching simply 'objectives'.

The characteristics of a good set of objectives can be summed up:[1]

1 The statement of objectives should describe both the kind of behaviour or understanding expected and the content or context to which the behaviour or understanding apply in this instance; for example, 'to think logically' is an objective that needs rooting in a context or set of contexts.
2 If an objective is complex, it needs to be stated analytically and specifically enough so that there is no doubt about what is expected.
3 Objectives should be so formulated that there are clear distinctions among the learning experiences required to attain the different behaviours. For example, knowledge about race does not itself necessarily develop a change of attitude towards race.
4 The objectives need to be conceived in terms of growth over a period of time, not as single goals.
5 They should be realistic, and include only what might possibly be achieved through classroom experience.
6 Finally, they should be, as far as is compatible with (5), broad enough to encompass what might reasonably be expected of the work of the team of teachers as part of the overall school objectives. I mean by this that care should be taken that important aspects of the needs of the pupil are not left out.

It is, of course, difficult to look at well-described objectives apart from the full scheme of work to which they are the statement of the theme. Here, however, are two examples worth studying.

The first is from a third-year, religious studies syllabus in a comprehensive school:

(i)   to equip the pupil with the concepts necessary for an understanding of the areas with which religion concerns itself, and the means, both in language and action, by which religion expresses itself and its particular interpretation of the world;
(ii) to help pupils towards an understanding of, and respect for, people whose beliefs and customs differ from their own;
(iii) to encourage pupils to probe and question received traditions, both Christian and non-Christian;

---

[1] A brief, clear and practical (if slightly mechanical) description of how to draw up aims and objectives will be found in Norman E. Gronlund, *Stating Behavioural Objectives for Classroom Instruction*, 2nd edn (West Drayton: Collier Macmillan, 1978).

(iv) to show pupils the contribution that religion has made to our culture.

No doubt that set of objectives could be faulted and improved, but it is a cogent and thoughtful, though commendably brief, statement, that clearly influenced the details of the syllabus that grew out of it.

Figure 7.1, in contrast, is another approach. This time not from a school, but from a published humanities scheme, setting out the objectives for three years' work.

I argue, then, that it is well worth spending time on the objectives of a syllabus. It is possible to ask one member of the team to draft an initial analysis, have it distributed to all members (and others whose views you need, such as the pastoral heads), inviting them to ponder the list for a few weeks. Then ask for alternative wordings, collate them, and redistribute them before a meeting to argue them out. That way you can effectively sharpen up the list of objectives.

Vertical continuity

A very different, but crucial aspect of a departmental syllabus is the vertical continuity, by which I mean the planning of learning sequences so that there is continuity up the years of the school. I suspect that in recent years, especially the turbulent teacher turnover years of the early and mid-1970s, we have over-emphasized continuity of teachers and under-emphasized continuity of teaching programmes. In many cases, of course, you cannot get continuity of teachers from year to year anyway, but in these circumstances, if not in all circumstances, continuity of programme is most important. This is one of the strongest aspects of curriculum planning in the USA, where it is usual to have a clear curriculum guide in each School District for each 'subject' from 'K through 12', that is from the earliest kindergarten years to the end of High School. It is, however, one of the weakest aspects of curriculum planning in the UK, with not only sharp discontinuities at each stage of schooling, but also from year to year in many junior schools, and from the lower school to the option years in most comprehensive schools — with an even sharper break at 16-plus before the sixth form.

At the very least there should be an awareness in each year of what has gone before, and the potential for future growth. A departmental syllabus should go further than that. There is an inevitable tension between the apparent needs of the pupil now, and the needs of his future learning. One function

Figure 7.1 Objectives for a humanities scheme [1]

Skills		Personal Qualities
Intellectual	*Social*	*Physical*	*Interests, Attitudes, Values*
1 The ability to find information from a variety of sources, in a variety of ways. 2 The ability to communicate findings through an appropriate medium. 3 The ability to interpret pictures, charts, graphs, maps, etc. 4 The ability to evaluate information. 5 The ability to organise information through concepts and generalisations. 6 The ability to formulate and test hypotheses and generalisations.	1 The ability to participate within small groups. 2 An awareness of significant groups within the community and the wider society. 3 A developing understanding of how individuals relate to such groups. 4 A willingness to consider participating constructively in the activities associated with these groups. 5 The ability to exercise empathy (i.e. the capacity to image accurately what it might be like to be be someone else).	1 The ability to manipulate equipment. 2 The ability to manipulate equipment to find and communicate information. 3 The ability to explore the expressive powers of the human body to communicate ideas and feelings. 4 The ability to plan and execute expressive activities to communicate ideas and feelings.	1 The fostering of curiosity through the encouragement of questions 2 The fostering of a wariness of overcommitment to one framework of explanation and the possible distortion of facts and the omission of evidence. 3 The fostering of a willingness to explore personal attitudes and values to relate these to other people's. 4 The encouraging of an openness to the possibility of change in attitudes and values. 5 The encouragement of worthwhile and developing interests in human affairs.

[1] Table from Alan Blyth, et al., *Place, Time and Society 8–13; Curriculum Planning in History, Geography and Social Science* (Collins/ESL Bristol for the Schools Council, 1976), p. 85. Reproduced by kind permission of Collins.

of the syllabus, which the teacher working on his own cannot achieve, is to reconcile that tension.

The key point is sequencing, and the question the head of department needs to ask is does the teaching look up the years, or does it settle for getting by for the present? For instance, is the method by which multiplication is taught at ages 7, 8 and 9 consistent with later needs? It is worth studying this example in some detail, for it illustrates the importance of sequential syllabus planning. It is possible to teach extremely well the so-called rule that you multiply by ten by 'adding a nought'. This appears to work splendidly when you are at the age when you have not met decimal fractions. So pupils multiply three by adding a nought, and get thirty. There are some teachers who teach that so clearly and so vigorously that the pupils learn it firmly. At a later stage in life, the pupil comes across a number like 2.3, and if you say, 'Can you multiply that by ten?', he looks delighted and replies: 'Two point three nought'! The teaching there shows a lack of sequencing. It is a syllabus that has not been thought out in terms of future needs. The axiom is that everything taught should be capable of future growth. A similar example is when teachers of younger secondary children call the full-stop 'a big pause'. Such an explanation may get you through that lesson or the next week or two, but it has no potential for the future understanding of language.

Many of the major concepts required by subjects in the later years of secondary schooling would be much improved with proper sequencing – for example, 'environment', 'contemporary', 'compatible', or 'development'. These are concepts which we throw at pupils later in schooling in ready-made words, because we have not in fact looked at the sequencing needs in departmental syllabuses.

A very careful analysis of the steps to growth is required, so that there is a sequencing, a preparation, and a deepening. There also has to be a consideration of the technically difficult point that the sequence has to be self-contained at two cut-off points, for those who leave a subject behind at the start of options, and those who do so at 16-plus. Instead I find that the first-year secondary syllabus is often a serendipity curriculum, with only an oblique relationship in skills, concepts and facts to the later stages. This is particularly so in various of the humanities syllabuses (for example, those geography syllabuses that move from Europe to North America, or history, starting with the remote past – 'the start of the world'), in English syllabuses (where sometimes there is little growth in reading ambitions from first to fourth years), in science syllabuses (where the reading and sequential deductions of fourth and fifth years are barely related to the work-card-based 'deduction' of the first years). In fact, the department needs to analyse the concepts, facts and skills required for later years, and ensure that these are there in the earlier years. Appendix 5 gives an example of a department attempting to list the skills required later in a way which indicates how the skills can be practised in the early years. Appendix 6 is somewhat more ambitious: library and non-narrative reading skills planned over the junior to secondary years. In this the aspects of the curriculum are analysed vertically, and the stages (not defined too sharply) horizontally. It is worth noting that the vocabulary of teaching is a syllabus aspect that requires consideration: pupils require at the least a consistent, developing approach to technical vocabulary, and preferably one in which there is a conscious awareness of the needs of later growth in earlier introductions. For instance (and the example is taken from Appendix 6), the technical names for parts of a book can be very confusing if used incorrectly (for alleged simplicity) in earlier stages — for example, 'cover', 'reference book'.

A careful study of the concepts required by a subject, and a placing of them in each year, so that the pupil meets them again and again in increasing complexity, is the vital stage in building up a vertical sequence in a scheme of work. Here, for instance, is part of the conceptual sequence that one school devised:

CONCEPTS	Year 1	Year 2	Year 3
Location	Absolute Location	Site	Site
	Site — Location of		Situation
	Settlement	Relative Location	Location of Industry
	Relative Location	Location of Shops	Location of Cities
	Location of Industry	Location of Port	Historical Location
		Location of Airport	
		Location of Industry	
		Consequences of	
		Location	
		Location of Types	
		of Agriculture	
Movement	Links	Distance — Straight	Connectivity
	Nodes	Line Distance	Attraction/Migration
		Time/Cost Distance	Congestion
	Distance — Type	Networks	Flows
	of Transport	Effect of Connectivity	Diffusion
	Networks	on Location	
	Frequency	Flows	
	Flows	Congestion	
	Congestion	Accessibility	
	Accessibility	Points of Interchange	
	Diffusion		

The concepts noted on the left are re-approached in each year in increasing complexity. Similar treatment was given to three other concepts which were felt to be important: distribution, systems (interaction), and change.[1]

A very clear example is in the projects expected in many humanities sessions. There is often a lack of modulation in the sequencing of 'research projects'. We tend to jump from the small 'closed' tasks ('In this encyclopaedia find the date of . . .') to the full-length assignment ('Here in the library are *x* thousand books; choose a subject, and you've got four weeks to finish it.')! It is no wonder that there are so many problems with CSE projects, A-level assignments, and university papers: we have not prepared a vertical continuity of syllabus approach.

Certainly there were times, and there probably are still schools, in which the opposite is the problem: the first-year secondary lessons are conceived virtually only as the first step on the long ascent towards a university honours course! For most of us though, the crucial problem is finding a way of making the first years of secondary school both valuable in themselves and including a properly prepared sequencing to later requirements.

The content

After all the preparation and analysis, what kinds of things should actually go into the scheme of work? The detailed form will clearly vary from subject to subject, but its outline will be broadly similar.

1 A detailed *statement of the objectives*, hierarchically arranged, with gradually increasing detail
2 Quotation of relevant *whole-school curriculum policies* to which the work of this team relates
3 Descriptions of *cognate subject teams*, on any work elsewhere in the school to which this department should relate
4 A list of the *key concepts, attitudes, and skills* that are necessary for the work of the department and will be taught by and practised within the department. These will not be arranged in pupil years, but in a logical and hierarchical system, for this is the underlying structure of the work. (Appendix 5 is an example of the section on attitudes

[1] The scheme was devised and taught at The Manor School, Cambridge, and is now published as Harrap's Basic Geography, Brian Greasley, et al., Harrap, 1979; the conceptual analysis is in the *Teaching Guide*, p. 5.

and skills from a secondary school's humanities scheme.) Alternatively it is sometimes possible to arrange this list so that it already starts to move towards a teaching scheme, by listing, for example, the skills along one axis of a grid, and the pupil years along another. Such an arrangement can show the main points of introduction and practice of major skills (though unless carefully done it risks going too soon to a year-by-year structure, and thus masking the logical structure). It is important to cover all the skills, not only those conventionally considered particular to your subject — for instance, reading needs consideration in both mathematics and science, not only in humanities and English.

5 *The topics to be covered.* The subject has to be taught to pupils via a series of 'topics', which can be thought of as a series of vehicles for carrying the objectives of the subject, and for exploring the concepts, developing the attitudes, and giving practice in the skills. The topics are likely to embody the facts necessary for the fulfilment of the objectives. Selecting the topics is likely to be a major task, for there are so many possibilities, so much that can be taught. It is therefore valuable to draw up at an early stage a list of criteria for topic selection. Here is one such list that I and a group of colleagues drew up:

Criteria for topic inclusion

In selecting topics and themes for the various years, the following criteria will be found useful:

(a) *Concept generation.* The usefulness of the topic or theme in helping the pupils grasp one of the fundamental concepts of the overall curriculum.

(b) *Direct relevance.* The usefulness of the content to the pupil's current or future life in this society.

(c) *Reference value.* The importance of the subject matter as containing references used commonly in the discourses of the world.

(d) *Contribution to the overall balance of examples.* The choice of each example should be considered from the point of view of the effect it has on the total presentation to the pupil. Certain eras, areas, or peoples must not be unwittingly presented in an inappropriate light. We should avoid reinforcing prejudices, stereotypes.

(e) *Pupil appeal.* The likely attractiveness of the subject matter, atmosphere and ideas to the adolescent Londoner.

(f) *Material availability.* The possibility of obtaining learning material of the appropriate levels and which is suitably attractive.

(g) *Teacher familiarity.* The extent to which normally trained teachers can work on this topic without undue expenditure of preparation time and without feeling too tentative.

In establishing an agreed list of topics, sufficient flexibility is required to allow teachers to flourish as individuals, but not to make the scheme no more than a suggestions list. For instance, one subject syllabus for a teaching year of forty weeks offered forty-two topics — each one of which could have taken between two and four weeks at a fairly conventional pace and with a reasonable degree of detail. Such a list is not a scheme of work. Finally, the topics must be so described that their relationship to the key concepts is brought out, and the opportunities for teaching and practising the main skills highlighted.

6 *Classroom approaches.* It is tempting to elevate 'method' above 'content', and many departmental schemes do that. Yet, if described correctly, the method must be subservient to the content, for the content is a list of what is being aimed at. Of course, there are times when 'the process is more important than the product', when it is how something is being done which is the main 'content' of the teaching sequence. This section of a scheme of work would wish to enable the teacher to develop his own style, but to assist with a discussion of methods concordant with the objectives, and of suggestions for the presentation of as many topics as possible.

7 *Learning resources.* From a consideration of objectives, content and method comes the selection of learning resources. Part of the method of selection is discussed in Chapter 4. Here it is sufficient to stress that the selection of learning materials is part of curriculum planning, and should therefore be an integral part of the drawing up of the scheme of work.

8 *Pupil reading lists.* In all subjects, there should be opportunities for pupils to continue their own pursuit of a topic by further study, and this usually involves further reading. There should therefore be carefully selected, and preferably annotated, lists of suitable books. These lists should, of course, be planned in conjunction with the school librarian or library service, and as far as possible it should be ensured that the books listed are available through the school library or bookshop.

9 *Professional reading.* The teachers should be encouraged to pursue their professional studies (as discussed in Chapter 4), and an annotated reading list should be included.

10 *Administration.* The final component of a scheme of work should be a succinct but complete outline of all aspects of departmental administration: stock, learning resources, equipment, procedures, pupil records, reports, teaching records, etc.

Processes

Although this book is addressed primarily to the head of department, and it is the holder of that post who is responsible for ensuring that the thinking is carried out and the document prepared, syllabus planning is a co-operative and collaborative process, and certainly not one in which the head of department returns from a summer holiday with multiple copies of a recently typed thesis. Indeed, the head of department's task is not 'drawing up' the syllabus, but 'drawing it out' of himself or herself and the team of other teachers.

Every situation will be different, and the process of syllabus planning will vary with it, but related to all is a series of steps which can be considered as necessary.

1 *Review*

Review the situation on: existing syllabuses; whole-school objectives; whole-school policies and syllabuses; related departmental syllabuses; public examination syllabuses and papers; subject literature; and syllabuses from other schools. This reviewing is a lengthy task that might take a group of teachers more than a term, and will no doubt be divided among team members, so that the work and the experience gained from it is shared. My impression is that too often the task of drafting is started too early and this important first stage hurried.

2 *Exploratory meetings*

Full meetings of the department or meetings of sub-groups then need to explore the implications. What are the particular characteristics of this department in this school? What have we learnt from other schools, from our whole-school objectives, from other departments in our school?

These meetings will include a great deal of unstructured discursive conversation. However, they must not be allowed to remain merely that: as points of principal emerge, the person in the chair should re-formulate them, and they should be minuted. Thus the end of the cycle of exploratory meetings will be recorded in a series of, perhaps terse, statements, at different levels of generality, but all useful in formulating policies.

3 *Drafting*

If the process has been thorough in its preliminaries, drafting emerges out of extensive thought. Obviously there are very many possible procedures, but the kind of sequence that could work would be to start by agreeing in full departmental meeting the structure of what is required, and allocating certain sections to individuals or sub-groups to work on for initial drafts. The possible contents list (pages 109–112) could be used as a basis. It is probably wise to have a crude overall decision in mind at this stage on the 'preliminaries' (sections (1) to (4), page 109) and the 'topics'. In my view it is normally essential to have a first draft of the preliminaries agreed before setting about the topics.

The agreement upon teaching sequences and the topics or activities which embody them, is considerably easier and educationally deeper the more thoroughly the preliminaries have been covered. I caution slowness at this stage, and the widest possible consultation, with submission to other heads of departments, any curriculum committee the school may have, the pastoral heads, the parents and the governors. Consultation with parents and governors is necessary both to gain the wisdom of their largely lay instinct and to ensure their support.

The outline of the teaching *content* having been established, a teaching *sequence* is now required. Again, full meetings are probably wise to discuss overall division into topics or activities, and then small sub-groups for detailed consideration of teaching units. It is easier for the sub-groups to draft such units if a common framework is agreed as a basis for each.

If there is any possibility during this process of a brief residential conference for those concerned (preferably with one or two advisers, such as the school's director of curriculum and a representative from the pastoral heads), it is to be highly recommended. Those of us working in the Inner London Education Authority have long benefited from such possibilities within its in-service training programme, and can speak warmly of the value of the work achieved. Indeed, one residential weekend, say from Friday dinner to Sunday lunch, can produce the equivalent of a year's after-school meetings – *and* keep those times free for preparation, follow-up, and detailed attention to subordinate sections.

Physical form

As no departmental scheme of work can or should be fixed in a permanent text, as it is likely to build up over quite a period of time, and as different sub-groups are likely to revise certain parts, a sectional loose-leaf format is probably the best. Obviously a clear and logical contents scheme is required, with lettered and numbered sections, rather than a continuously numbered page sequence. It is worth establishing a proper layout grid, and having all re-typing done to the same specifications, for ease of continuous reading. It should hardly need stressing that the typing must be professionally done, and the proofs carefully checked. Unfortunately very many school departmental syllabuses are very poor examples of layout, typing and proof correcting!

Have sufficient copies run off, with spares for store. It is too easy to forget parent committees, inspectors, governors, pastoral heads, student teachers — and future members of all those categories!

Using the scheme of work

A head of department has only himself to blame if the much laboured-over scheme of work becomes merely shelf clutter. Presuming that it was conceived of and drafted as a working document, it must be used as such. The head of department should use it:

1 For induction of student teachers and probationers
2 Briefing of part-time and extra departmental teachers
3 For departmental reviews of aspects of the team's work
4 For individual professional development and career appraisal
5 For in-school evaluation.

Finally, of course, it should be part of a revision process even before it is completed, for a departmental scheme of work has to grow, expand and adjust, and act as the stimulus for the teacher team's continuing professional growth.

Conclusion

In the autonomous UK school, curriculum planning is largely school based. In this the head of department is the key figure, contributing to the whole-school curriculum plans, and drawing out from them his own facet. The scheme of work — syllabus, curriculum guide, instrument of policy, or book of the department — is the vehicle for this curriculum planning and the means whereby the daily class teaching is given a significance and power beyond what the individual teacher could normally generate on his own.

This then is one of the major responsibilities of a head of department, requiring the skills of analysis, perception, group leadership, drafting, negotiating and organizing. The processes require knowledge of pupils, staff, the field of education, the particular subject, and the community. Ensuring that there is an adequate scheme of work may not be the first or even the most burdensome part of the head of department's task, but it is a central one for the British head of department, and it is a crucial part of his leadership. Indeed it could be said that the quality of curriculum planning by heads of department is the test of the faith that our country has in school-based curriculum planning. The evidence does not suggest that it is a trust that has been carried out as professionally as we should like — and whether or not this curriculum planning will be left in the hands of schools depends partly on whether we can improve it.

8 The head of department and library and study skills

Ann Irving

The development of library research and study skills in pupils is an important one for heads of department for two main reasons. First, the ability to find and use information cannot be related to one or two subjects because it is the substance of *all* studying. It is, therefore, the province of *all* heads of department. Secondly, the teaching of a particular subject in today's world is the teaching of the *study* of that subject, and so every teacher is a teacher of reading and study. The head of department's responsibility revolves round his ability to help his staff work as a team within the department and with other departmental teams — a particularly crucial task, for library research and study skills are across-the-curriculum skills, as essential to the business of learning as reading and writing. It has been said that the head of department's task is one of continuous tension:

> There is a continuous tension in the Head of Department's task — arguably more tension than in the post of head teacher itself . . . the tension comes from the problem of balance: balance between the overall school requirements and the narrower subject needs; between organizational possibilities and theoretical ideas; between flexibility and rigidity; between teacher and teacher; between pupils and teachers . . . between long-term planning and today's problems.[1]

Balance is perhaps where the library or resource centre can exert most influence, by allowing pupils to cross boundaries between subjects or make links between them. But the library cannot do this alone. Users need to have the skills which turn libraries into active learning centres, laboratories where the skills of studying are developed and practised under the guidance of teacher and librarian in harmony. To examine the head of department's role in the process of learning how to learn through library resources, it is first necessary to consider what library and study skills are, and who should

[1] Michael Marland, *Head of Department* (Heinemann Educational Books, 1971).

possess them, before examining the likely administrative and human factors which might affect the application of that role.

Library research and study skills

A growing number of people believe that our expanding body of knowledge necessitates more independent learning in schools: Education is concerned with the transmission of knowledge and skills. But it is also concerned with transmitting a love of knowledge, and the skills that are required for the independent pursuit of knowledge.'[1] Many of these skills are used when seeking knowledge in libraries, but it should not be assumed that they are peculiar to either the library or the classroom; they are the same skills, and are the basis of all school work: 'There are no library skills, *per se*, only study skills. All study skills are the shared responsibility of all who teach and should be an integral part of the planned, on-going classroom teaching and learning programme.'[2] Library skills are, therefore, only a part of study skills — each dependent upon the other if the learning process is to be effective and efficient. And they need to be taught to pupils within the context of their curricular subjects in addition to any instruction given in the library.

A recent investigation[3] into the range and nature of the skills needed for using library resources involved teachers, librarians and pupils who were interviewed about the skills thought to be necessary. The broadest definition of study skills included all those used for the gathering and use of information in order to gain new knowledge. The sources of information include books, journals, slides, tapes, objects or artefacts, people and places, television, radio, and the newer sources of information conveyed by computers — Prestel, Ceefax and Oracle. Thus the skills for using them are broader than those traditionally associated with printed resources. The range is also wide; from defining what information is needed through to choosing the most suitable method of presentation.

The skills identified during the investigation fell into five broad groups.

[1] Eric Lunzer and Keith Gardner (eds), *The Effective Use of Reading* (Heinemann Educational Books for the Schools Council, 1979).

[2] Ruth Ann Davies, *The School Library Media Center: a Force for Educational Excellence* 2nd edn (Ann Arbor: Bowker, 1974).

[3] Ann Irving and Wilfrid Snape, *Educating Library Users in Secondary Schools*, British Library Research and Development Department Report no. 5467 (British Library Research and Development Department, 1979).

1 *Finding items in the library*

Understanding the structures of knowledge through the classification scheme, and establishing the relationships between them through the use of the catalogues. A knowledge of the keywords or synonyms used to describe the subject so that searching is facilitated.

2 *Finding information in books and other resources*

Knowing how to make use of a contents list, index and sub-headings and employing appropriate reading strategies (for example, skimming and scanning) to locate relevant sections quickly. Understanding that the contents list indicates the author's arrangement, while the index offers alternative arrangements for accessing the information, based on a selection of what is relevant or needed. Advanced reading strategies are developed so that pupils can practise the 'gutting' of texts with confidence.

3 *Making notes*

Noting only those points which will help to meet the information needs expressed and defined by the pupil, and being able to organize them for easy retrieval later (for example, by using index cards, loose-leaf folders, etc.). Understanding the need for taking sufficient notes that will mean something when consulted at a later date.

4 *Evaluating information*

Questioning the authority of sources, asking which one is correct, if any, and what thoughts have been provoked in the pupil during the process of synthesis.

5 *Presentation*

Understanding the purpose of the assignment so that presentation can be properly organized to meet the perceived ends. An awareness of what 'writing in their own words' really means, and when to paraphrase, when to quote, etc. Pupils are not often clear in their own minds about the purpose of personal expression when most of their thinking about books has been concerned with their authority and excellence. The final presentation, be it essay or project, should be structured and guided according to a plan devised by the pupil in the light of his knowledge and understanding of the topic, the purpose of the assignment, and the target audience.

Skills for whom?

There were many similarities in the responses from different subject teachers interviewed during the investigation, leading to the conclusion that the research and study skills identified

were needed by all pupils for all subjects. Levels of sophistication would differ between age-groups as would the
range of skills, but some development of study skills seems
applicable to all subjects — sciences, humanities, even the
practical subjects of art and crafts. Others would agree
that 'the teaching of a particular subject is the teaching
of the study of that subject, and that makes inescapable
the fact that every teacher is a teacher of reading and study.'[1]
And for those who doubt the need for the skills to be gained
by *all* pupils in comprehensive schools:

> We award the highest academic accolade to a student who can
> see a question, focus it into an enquiry, trace sources, find relevant
> information in those sources, collate the information, reorganize
> that information in a way that meets the question posed, and
> write up the reorganized material as a report. To those who achieve
> that pinnacle of scholarship we award a Ph.D. This same process is
> the one we have adopted as the main teaching method for the less
> academic and less well motivated school pupil.[2]

A CSE project encompasses all the research and study
skills so far discussed, and is perhaps the most difficult
assignment to complete successfully for any pupil, of whatever ability — and yet, the art is largely untaught.

It is clear, therefore, that library research and study
skills do relate to the total school programme. Elsewhere
in this book the role of the head of department is considered in relation to the overall curriculum planning, and
to the processes involved in drawing up a scheme of work.
A link between the two themes may be made by considering some of the administrative problems and human factors
which the head of department might encounter during
deliberations on library research and study skills.

Administrative problems and solutions

There are three main points to be considered by the head of
department wishing to co-ordinate the teaching and development of library skills: the materials available, assignments set
for pupils which require them to be used, and the development of the skills themselves.

---

[1] A. S. Artley, 'Effective study — its nature and nurture', in J. Allen (ed.),
Forging Ahead in Reading (Newark: International Reading Association, 1968).
[2] Michael Marland, et al., *Language Across the Curriculum: The Implementation of the Bullock Report in the Secondary School* (Heinemann Educational
Books, 1977).

1 *Materials*

Material must be available in the library to back up the department's teaching. So often the main textbook refers to other items which no one has bothered to obtain, and pupils wishing to broaden their reading are frustrated when their motivation to find out more is high. Many pupils do not have, even today, other resources to draw upon outside school, and are put at a disadvantage before they can begin to develop sound study habits. It is the head of department's responsibility to ensure that material is made available and accessible to all pupils by encouraging teachers to check on resources before setting assignments.

One solution to the problem of knowing what quantity exists is to ask the librarian, either in school or in local public libraries, to produce a resources guide showing how much material the library possesses on the topics likely to be studied by most pupils — the popular topics covered every year for example (see Figure 8.1). If the department decides to cover a topic for which there are insufficient resources in school, then the local public library service can usually provide 'project collections' for long periods, when required. If nothing can be obtained at pupil level, then the department can consider making its own materials.

But materials are still not accessible in the library unless the library is clearly guided so that pupils know where to look. It seems a simple statement to make but there are many libraries where only the staff or librarians know where to find relevant items. Much can be done to make libraries less daunting for the young pupil; large, clear labels over shelves and a clear wall plan are two easy ways to help.

It is also worth noting that materials can both support and influence the curriculum, as the recent controversies over racism and sexism in children's books has shown. Every teacher needs to keep abreast of what is being published in his or her subject so that the material in the library stands a chance of balancing all the relevant views and theories.

2 *Assignments*

What is taught in a department is obviously based upon agreement — a balance — between staff, overall school aims and philosophy, and the examination syllabus chosen by the school. How the teaching is done is another matter, and the setting of assignments that demand pupils' information-handling skills is a most neglected activity. If not neglected, it is often misdirected: 'Aimless trots through catalogues and reference books, by pupils carrying work cards or slips of typed

Figure 8.1 Example of library resources guide

COMMUNITY – USE OF RESOURCE CENTRE

OUR STOCK WILL BE SUPPLEMENTED BY A PROJECT COLLECTION SELECTED BY THE COUNTY LIBRARY.
SEE ALSO THE SEPARATE LIST OF FILMS ON THE LOWER SCHOOL NOTICE BOARD.

SUBJECT	DEWEY NUMBER	TYPE OF MATERIAL AVAILABLE	AMOUNT OF RESOURCES AVAILABLE
ADVERTISING	SEE SHOPPING 658.87	BOOKS, OLD MAGAZINES FOR CUTTING UP	NOT MANY BOOKS AVAILABLE
HEDGEROW STUDY	SEE BIOLOGY 574 BIRDS 598.2	BOOKS, FILMSTRIP 'KNOW THE LAND' BOOKS, PAMPHLETS, CHARTS, ILLUSTRATIONS	PLENTY AVAILABLE
	ANIMALS 591/599	BOOKS, PAMPHLETS, CHARTS, SLIDES ILLUSTRATIONS	SEE ALSO 'ENCYCLOPAEDIA OF NATURE AND SCIENCE' AND
	PLANTS/FLOWERS 580/582	BOOKS, CHARTS	'THE INTERNATIONAL
	TREES/LEAVES 582	BOOKS, CHARTS, PAMPHLETS	WILDLIFE ENCYCLOPAEDIA'
DEVELOPMENT OF WRITING	SEE WRITING 411 ANCIENT HISTORY 930 COMMUNICATION 384	BOOKS, JACKDAW, SLIDES BOOKS BOOKS	FOUR OR FIVE BOOKS QUITE A FEW BOOKS QUITE A FEW BOOKS
MORSE CODE	SEE CODES 652.8	BOOKS, ENCYCLOPAEDIAS	ONE OR TWO BOOKS

(Handout produced by Harry Carlton Comprehensive School, East Leake, Nottinghamshire)

paper, setting them questions to answer, which nobody apart from a desperate teacher-librarian, would ever think to ask.'[1]

Assignments should be constructed so that they offer pupils not only knowledge of the subject but also knowledge of the study of that subject, and this requires a clear understanding of what purpose lies behind the work set:

> Research work on topics and assignments is really only of value if it leads to the acquisition of knowledge that the children want, and answers questions that they are asking themselves. Too often it appears to a child that information is being sought solely for the benefit of the teacher.[2]

The head of department can encourage and co-ordinate the setting of library-based assignments after consideration of subjects within the department and what staff wish pupils to learn about them. Then learning assignments may be created that will be currently relevant and potentially useful for the future; assignments that will develop the skills for finding and using information through the curriculum, through the syllabus, rather than simply added on to a library exercise. The only thing that many pupils learn from doing library assignments and exercises is how to do library assignments and exercises; they do not readily transfer the skills to other academic work. As an example, the following questions from worksheets designed to give pupils practice at finding information show how difficult such transfer would be:

> If you had just read *The Celebrated Jumping Frog of Calaveras County*, which brought fame to its author in 1865, where would you go to find information about the life of the author?
>
> If you wanted to read the North Atlantic Treaty, April, 1949, which book would give it in full text?
>
> If you had to determine the correctness of the grammar used in a theme on 'Dependency Characteristic of Rats' which of these handbooks would best serve your needs?
>
> If you had to determine the author of 'And what is so rare as a day in June' which of these books would confirm your guess or answer your question?

and a final question designed to test pupils' ability to use a dictionary:

> In one paragraph, comment on the possibility of Samuel Johnson's success in attaining this aim: 'I have laboured to refine our language to grammatical purity, and to clear it from colloquial barbarisms, licentious idioms, and irregular combinations.'

[1] Norman Beswick, *Resource-Based Learning* (Heinemann Educational Books, 1977).
[2] Anthony Kamm and Boswell Taylor, *Books and the Teacher* (University of London Press [now Dunton Green: Hodder & Stoughton Educational], 1966).

Far better is to design assignments that fall naturally into a course of studies, but which require skilful use of library materials. And care should be taken to ensure that the task is humanly possible, unlike this example: 'Accurately draw, then describe, the solar system.'

3 Skills development

The skills concerned are the same research skills used by scientists in industry, sixth-formers studying for GCE A-level examinations, CSE project students, and the local community group wishing to express its views about a new motorway:

topic definition
assessment of information need
search strategy
analysis
usage.

It may be helpful to expand on some of these stages a little — for example, topic definition and search strategy.

Topic definition involves a process of self-questioning. What *is* the subject (its title; the aspect or approach to be made; the boundaries of it; the purpose of the assignment; the audience; the language of the subject, the keywords or synonyms used to describe it)? What do I know already about this subject? What do I need to find out about it in order to complete the work (compiling a 'shopping list' of information needed)? Where do I start looking (which resources: people, places, libraries, books, etc.)? The whole of this stage should take place *before* a library is approached. It helps to clarify the extent of existing knowledge and understanding, the extent of the assignment set, its purpose and therefore possible structure, and the range of information required properly listed under appropriate search terms — essential knowledge for searching any index.

Search strategy involves moving from the general to the specific, starting with sources which will provide an overview of the topic and leading towards material that will provide information on the topic in more detail. Encyclopaedias offer a general introduction; a list of contents makes the general approach whereas the index offers a more specific body of knowledge about all aspects of the topic culled from many articles relating to it. The search skills include:

alphabetization — to several letters
scanning — quick look for facts on a page
skimming — reading only the most relevant paragraphs

notemaking — noting relevant points that will help to complete the assignment

reviewing — establishing whether or not enough information has been gathered.

The weighting factors to be borne in mind during the search include a consideration of time, resources available and length. It is pointless to undertake a lengthy and sophisticated search for information if the material is difficult to obtain, the completed assignment is to be 1000 words long and there is only one week in which to complete it.

How, then, does the head of department help pupils develop the skills? There are three procedures which will aid the department in this process:

1 Identify the skills needed within the department. Some will have particular relevance and others will be widely applicable. For example, using the index to a book and scanning pages for facts will be generally applicable to all subjects, while handling gazetteers and interpreting flow diagrams may be specific to certain subjects.

2 Decide when to teach a skill specifically and who should do so. This is not to suggest that any one person should teach study skills but that responsibilities for teaching them should be clearly defined. All staff must support and reinforce this by reminding pupils of the skills, and setting assignments which require them to be practised.

3 Make sure that all staff understand what is being done. The work done by Gibbs[1] offers a useful and practical strategy. Or the head of department could ask staff to research a project they have set for pupils so that all can experience the frustration and begin to discern solutions. Sharing the problems of pupils is a very humane way to approach teaching in this area.

The human factors

The head of department is a manager of his department's resources, and managing anything or anyone means blending different needs, abilities and personalities with what resources are available — balancing the tensions. There are several groups of people with an interest in the development of study skills; headteachers, assistant teachers, other heads of department, librarians, the pupils, ancilliary and other school staff.

[1] Graham Gibbs, *Learning to Study: A Guide to Running Group Sessions* (Milton Keynes: Institute for Educational Technology, The Open University, 1977).

Headteachers

In a sense, headteachers will have the least involvement in any study skills programme because their job involves keeping governors, parents and the education authority reasonably happy. Their support will be valuable, but it may not be essential to the successful implementation of departmental policy. (It has been said that innovation is never successfully transmitted downwards.)

Assistant teachers

An immediate reaction from some teachers to a proposal for the teaching of study skills is that it is unnecessary — nobody taught *them*; or that their pupils are already bright enough and do not need extra teaching. It may be necessary to point out that in further and higher education there has been a great deal of study skills instruction, even in universities, where the brightest pupils are sent. It is possible, with a good memory, to complete school education successfully, but it is not possible for all but a few pupils to study effectively so that they know how to learn in any situation, and learn with some enjoyment and therefore high motivation. The difficulty which many pupils experience while studying may be compared with the frustration of the slow reader whose pleasure is thwarted by stumbling attempts to decode the words of the story. A substantial part of learning should be enjoyable.

Some teachers would endorse this: 'To be able to use a library is a necessary part of being an efficient student'[1] and it is practical to start with such teachers, hoping that their enthusiasm, example and help will spread to others.

Heads of department

Other heads of department are more difficult to contend with because most people see their specialisms as unique. It may be profitable to refer them to the whole-school approaches outlined in *Language Across the Curriculum*[2] and to the bulky literature on the need to teach pupils how to study — for school and beyond. Although most of the effort has been directed at the more academic students, recent work has been aimed at less academic pupils and their needs for information in everyday life.[3] Some opposition may come from science

---

[1] Ann Irving and Wilfred Snape, *Educating Library Users in Secondary Schools*, op. cit.

[2] Michael Marland, op. cit.

[3] Terence Brake, *The Need to Know*, British Library Research and Development Department Report no. 5511 (British Library Research and Development Department, 1980).

departments where laboratory work is seen as the prime method for learning, and where the need for greater independent searching for information is considered inappropriate because there is a set body of knowledge to be learned. The problem here is that the body of basic scientific knowledge is rapidly expanding — the literature of physics is now doubling in six years — and selections must be made during the seven years of secondary education if the teaching is to be up to date. Scientists outside school recognize the need to be able to search for and evaluate information quickly and effectively if expensive duplication of research is to be avoided. It has been shown that certain products have been reported as 'discovered' when the literature in previous years had already reported the discovery.

Librarians

Although hardly mentioned so far, librarians are key people and 'experts in the techniques of learning from books' who should be 'charged with the responsibility for promoting the developing of such techniques by others'.[1] There are few professional librarians in secondary schools in Britain, (about 600 in fact when there are around 8000 secondary schools), but librarians with special responsibilities for children and schools are attached to most public library systems. They are a valuable and largely untapped resource and their daily work demonstrates a sophisticated development of research and study skills. They can also assess readability levels and suggest suitable items on most topics whether printed, aural or visual. Librarians who do work in schools are often unable to demonstrate these abilities fully because of their different conditions of service — for example, many are allowed only half an hour for lunch, no relief staffing when they might attend departmental meetings or be released for in-service training, they work office hours, and are usually employed to work for forty-nine weeks so that they do not have the recuperation periods enjoyed by their teaching colleagues, despite their qualifications being equivalent, and sometimes greater, than other staff. Many schools with professional librarians prevent them from acting out this key role by denying them relief staffing and also clerical assistance — it does seem a waste!

The other kind of librarian in schools is the teacher-librarian, somehow expected to run an efficient service in a few 'free'

[1] Ernest Roe, *Teachers, Librarians and Children* (St Albans: Crosby Lockwood, 1965).

periods each week, despite the recommendations of the Bullock Committee for the job to be a full-time one. A library cannot operate as a learning laboratory where research and study skills are practised under expert guidance and supervision when it is only open occasionally and staffed inadequately, and when the teacher-librarian can be taken away to fill in for teachers' absences. The professional librarian at least has the advantage of being *always* a librarian; a resource always accessible for teachers and pupils. The library itself is a mixed-ability learning resource.

Pupils

Pupils are the most likely beneficiaries from any planned study skills programme. Little is known about how they learn or what is learned in the long term. Skinner[1] pinpointed the problem when he suggested that 'education is what survives when what has been learned has been forgotten' which seems a strong argument for concentrating on the art of studying rather than the content.

Ancilliary staff

Ancilliary staff are a very important school resource particularly when in the form of clerical assistance in the library. There is no point in appointing a professional librarian, or a teacher-librarian, who then spends most of the time doing clerical work, often badly or inefficiently. The head of department is concerned with making the best use of resources, and in contributing to the school's objectives and priorities. Where these are clearly defined it will be obvious that clerical support is essential and time-saving, and permits professional specialisms to be practised. If a school librarian is often seen typing catalogue cards, it may be worth asking if that time would be better spent working with pupils and teachers towards the development of research and study skills which will lead to efficient study habits, better school work and more confident pupils.

Other school staff

Another valuable resource for the head of department to draw upon is the remedial or compensatory department, if one exists. Like librarians, remedial teachers are experts in the techniques of reading and study, encouraging the use of

[1] B. F. Skinner in *New Scientist*, 21 May 1964, p. 484.

resources, developing the skills and fostering them through support and guidance.

Since librarians and remedial teachers deal with children across subject disciplines and across ability levels it is perhaps appropriate to have them attend all head of department and curriculum planning meetings. They are the most familiar with study problems and possible solutions, picking up the pieces after other teachers have given up, and in many cases doing so successfully.

The human factors are diverse and complex but the head of department can bring a range of specialisms together for the benefit of all the teachers in the department. The specialisms exist inside school and outside it, and they are practical and valuable to those who can see a need for them. They could be used effectively if invited to participate in syllabus planning and may help to alleviate some of the common problems experienced in comprehensive school education. The problems of expanding knowledge, mixed-ability teaching, and scarce resources can be counterbalanced by emphasizing independence in learning and studying, and this must imply specific planning for the teaching of the necessary skills.

A look to the future

The overall theme of this chapter has been that every teacher's responsibility extends to the teaching of the study of his subject, as well as the content. Learning to study is an essential part of the whole curriculum, and teaching the skills for lifelong learning are surely what schools are for. The skills concerned are those commonly known as research skills; although they differ in sophistication between age-groups, the range is the same, from the initial definition of a topic or inquiry through to the organization of the information gathered and its initial use for essays or projects. Long-term use cannot be precisely estimated, but our developing technology renders it potentially invaluable. Computers will have a profound effect on society. Knowledge of the world is growing at a rate faster than ever before because previous limitations to the development of new knowledge are diminishing — machines can perform feats faster and more efficiently than people and problems can now be solved, hypotheses tested and information processed very quickly. Material can be stored very cheaply and sent on-line almost anywhere in the world. The way we learn to handle information will determine the way people live, work and communicate in the future,[1] and the ability and determination of teachers to participate in teaching the skills to successive generations will be a measure of their understanding of the educational process in a rapidly developing society. The following quotation summarizes the sentiment behind this chapter and the rationale for it: 'In large measure study skills are the most permanent and most useful of all learnings; facts will change, but how to deal efficiently, effectively, creatively and honestly with facts will not change.'[2]

---

[1] Norman Longworth, ' "Information" in secondary-school curricula', M.Phil. thesis (Southampton University, 1976).

[2] Ruth Ann Davies, *The School Library Media Center: A Force for Educational Excellence*, op. cit.

9 Developing reading

Colin Harrison

'When brain meet book it dread'

This chapter is about the problems of developing reading in school. It concentrates on secondary level, and in particular on the problems of a head of department. I want to deal with these problems under four headings. First, the business of choosing the texts that we use in school; secondly, the reading tasks that we give to children; thirdly, the issue of staff development, and how we can organize that vis-à-vis reading in our department; fourthly, but most importantly, the children themselves, and what we can do to make their reading more effective.

Choosing texts

It is not necessarily the case that when we talk about choosing *texts* we mean choosing *books*. This is one problem. The Schools Council Effective Use of Reading Project[1], of which I was a member of the project team, did a survey of the reading materials in use in a large number of schools over one week, and found that many of the materials were not books at all — they were worksheets. Children also read from the blackboard, and there were many other types of printed materials that came into school, including magazines, brochures and newspapers. A survey of the difficulty level of those texts was made, and we were rather disturbed by what we found. To begin with, we discovered that the difficulty level of texts in use with first-year children was not significantly different from the difficulty level that we found in the materials at fourth-year level.

[1] The report of the project was published as *The Effective Use of Reading*, ed. Eric Lunzer and Keith Gardner (Heinemann Educational Books for the Schools Council, 1979).

We also looked at the problems of choosing materials, and this is one specific area of concern in relation to the role of a head of department. It turns out that as individuals we are rather unreliable in determining how difficult a text is likely to be. I say 'unreliable', and I am using the term in its statistical sense. One person, even if he has a fair amount of experience, might very well get a rather different opinion or set of results from another. So what can we do? Am I saying that an average teacher is likely to be unable to choose books for children? No, it is rather that in this specific matter of deciding what reading level a book is likely to have, at what age an average child is likely to be able to cope, it turns out that we tend not to agree with each other very much at all. However, when different teachers have their opinions pooled then a much more stable picture emerges. So what I want to argue for is the pooling of ideas in departmental meetings, the sharing of ideas when books are being chosen for a course, and when decisions are being made about buying a book or producing worksheets. Of course, this will take up time, but I submit that unless we build it in as part of departmental meeting procedure, then we are likely to continue to be inaccurate in getting books that are appropriate for children's needs.

There are three terms which I think can be useful in helping us to decide whether a book is appropriate or not, and these are used quite often in the American literature on reading. They refer to whether a book is being used at the *instructional* level, at the *independent* level, or at a child's *frustration* level, and I think these terms are quite useful in helping us to differentiate between the kinds of gain a child might make from his reading. The independent level is when a child is able to work on his own, without the teacher's direct support, perhaps in project work or topic work or when he is doing research. Now in these circumstances research on readability of texts has suggested that materials ought to be one, or preferably two, years easier in terms of their reading level than materials that are used at the instructional level. The instructional level is when a child is able to cope with his reading materials, provided that the teacher is giving some specific help, or is at least present and able to give some specific help if it is needed. If the child is still not able to cope, then this would be described as frustration level. It might be worthwhile asking whether we make that kind of differentiation within our own departments. Are we aware which books are likely to be causing most problems? Are we aware when a child is able to work independently from our own textbooks?

One of the problems we found in the readability survey came when we asked the question: 'Are the books that are used for homework easier than the books that tend to be used in class?' On the American view we would say that the books used for homework ought to be two years easier in terms of difficulty level precisely because there is no teacher around to help. What we found was the exact opposite. It turned out that the more difficult a book is, the more likely it is that it is going to be used for homework. The reason is that in science, for example, the hard-pressed science teacher has enough of a problem trying to get the laboratory work covered and the notes for the writing-up of an experiment done during the lesson, together with some blackboard work. There is just no time left to look at the course book that accompanies the practical work. So what the teacher understandably says is, 'Look at the textbook to help you with your homework and to help you do the questions in the exercise.' But as teachers we have a professional responsibility to see that our reading materials are used to the best effect. It seems to me that we must accept the need to build into lessons more explicitly the use of these fairly dense and difficult texts. I am thinking here of subject areas such as chemistry, physics and biology, but in our readability survey we also found that in the social sciences and humanities field, in history, geography, and especially geology, there were very difficult and dense texts, and teachers were not able to find the time in the classroom to explicate and help children with them. My own feeling was that this led many teachers to feel that they could not expect much from children so far as using books was concerned. I would argue that our expectations might be raised if we were able to bring more shared attention to books into class time, so that children were put in a position where they could grapple with dense texts when the teacher was around to help.

Another strategy on our survey was to ask the children what their opinions were of their reading materials. We found for a start that the children were no less reliable judges of difficulty than the teachers; indeed, their estimates of difficulty level correlated very highly with those of the teachers. I think this corresponds with our own experience; we tend to feel children are pretty shrewd judges of whether they are understanding or not, a good part of the time at any rate. So I think it is quite reasonable to ask the children what their opinion is of a textbook.

Some teachers have encouraged children to rewrite their own science texts in language that other children could understand, and have gone on to make a very useful analysis of the kind of changes that they made. For example, where the text said: 'Obtain a bone from your local butcher', the children would say: 'Get a bone from the butcher — if you can!'. So there was more energy in their writing, and this made quite a significant difference. If there is some life in the writing it increases motivation, and there is no doubt at all that if motivation is increased then a child's level of reading can increase as well. What I am saying is that we should look for ways to develop and heighten motivation and if getting children to help write is one, then let us try it.

Another approach could be to ask children, at the end of a particular segment of a course, to rewrite the worksheet that they have just done so that another set of children could do it more effectively. You do not in this case have the problem of the conceptual content being diminished; the aim is to get over certain instructions to help the children do an experiment or a task, and communication is what is important.

One of the schools we worked with on the Effective Use of Reading Project had a 'Worksheet Workshop', and this might be worth considering. The school had a committee of about half a dozen teachers, and two children from each age-group from first year to fourth year, and met in a lunch-hour with worksheets from a whole range of different subject areas. The group looked very closely at these and they talked about which were well presented, or poorly presented, which ones were effective and which ones looked most interesting. It perhaps will not surprise you to learn that the English department came out rather poorly and the image of the English specialist slaving over a hot Banda during assembly was stoutly maintained by this exercise. The geographers, who tend to be rather more highly organized, fared much better; their materials were far more carefully thought out and prepared.

Reading tasks

In this section I want to put a major emphasis on reading tasks because I am not at all sure it is something to which we have given enough attention. In the Bullock Report[1] one of the most important emphases so far as reading is concerned is the concept of *purpose*. Why is it that children are being asked to do a particular kind of reading?

Very often the tasks might be highly specific, but this is not necessarily good teaching. In our classroom observation

---

[1] Department of Education and Science, *A Language for Life* (HMSO, 1975).

work on the Effective Use of Reading Project what we began to wonder was whether children were being offered tasks which allowed them to develop their reading skills. We were not looking at the problems of failing readers. We were looking at the opportunities presented to children who could read to develop and extend their reading. The kind of situation we encountered could be exemplified through considering what we found in one humanities department in a comprehensive school. There was a very interesting integrated humanities course being run with first- and second-formers, and some extremely able teachers were working on it; there was no doubt about that. But when we came to examine the booklet they had produced, we found that the reading tasks tended to run something like this:

> Turn to pages 41 and 42 of (a reference book) and answer this question: How did early man obtain his food?

The next question would be:

> Write all you can about the socialization of early man using (another reference book) pages 51 and 54.

I sympathize with teachers who feel that many children would not be capable of using a book independently at first-year level to find that information for themselves. But we must realize that the children were not being offered a basis for developing that kind of research skill in the task as it was presented. The task required a reading of fairly short, specific sections, and the children were doing no more than summarizing these, or even quoting verbatim in order to answer the questions.

What I would argue for, difficult though it is, is much more attention to developing research skills on a sequential basis, and I think this can be done. I have visited a junior school where 10- and 11-year-olds were perfectly capable of working independently from reference books. How had they been taught? One of the things that had happened was that they had learnt to acquire a vocabulary which gave them control over their reading. They were able to use terms like 'skim' and 'scan' and to use this knowledge to help them to vary their approaches to different texts. *Skimming* means flipping through something to get a general idea, and *scanning* is simply looking for a specific word, phrase, or a date. These 11-year-olds used that vocabulary, and they were able to describe what they were doing much more effectively than an average fourth-year could in secondary school. Most children do not have a basis for describing their reading behaviour; most teachers could not do it either. But if what we are wanting to do is to give the children more conscious control over how they tackle their reading, then this is a very important issue. It relates to my earlier point that reading tasks are important, in that they must be structured to try to offer children this kind of opportunity.

I want to say a word about vocabulary because on the reading project teachers repeatedly told us that helping children to cope with difficult vocabulary was one of their major problems. Heads of department also reported that this was their biggest single problem at CSE and GCE O-level. One of the interesting approaches that we found in our school visits was at a school in the Manchester area where a head of department had begun by inviting children to say, at the end of a year's course, which words they had found difficult. If you imagine asking your second years in chemistry, say, what words they found difficult in their course, you might get a very different answer from the ones that you would come up with yourselves as a department. It could be that you would be thinking of a concept such as *molecule*, whereas for a child it might be a much more straightforward word like *salt*, or *solution*, which happens to be used differently in another part of the curriculum. It might be something as simple as *rubber* or *rubber band*, or *elastic*, which we found in another context was causing some children difficulties in physics. What the teacher was able to do was to work from those word lists and to compile glossaries which were then hung up in the laboratory. The children could go over and consult them when they had a problem, and the advantage of this was that it could be done on a year-by-year basis. You could do this for each year group and you could then have a word list hung up in the laboratory on the basis of the previous class's ideas which could be potentially very valuable.

Another topic in relation to reading tasks that I want to stress is the concept of rejecting a book. A recent British Library survey has confirmed that, if we do any library work at all, it tends to be along the lines of teaching children how to select a book. I would argue that it is equally important to teach a child how to reject a book. Very often we complain that a child doing topic work, for example, will include arbitrary facts because they had a tangential connection with his original subject, and there was some overlap of terms in a book's index. So I would want to encourage children to be made more aware of the importance of rejecting a book that they feel is not for them, and to stress that this might quite often be the case.

The Effective Use of Reading Project did some time-lapse

cine work into children's use of school libraries. What we found was very interesting. The first point to note is that the Dewey system, on which most school libraries are based, was not used very much at all. This came as something of a painful surprise to me because I have made my contribution to a department's work as a librarian and am aware of how much time it takes to update the classification system. Much time is spent in the library indexing and classifying books and completing cards on them. By the time we had done this research we came to feel that this time was not really profitably spent. At sixth-form level perhaps it is essential, but lower down, even in the fourth year, what happens? A child goes to the index and pulls out a drawer of cards, and he is busy flipping through in order to decide whether the library holds any books on genetics. He has to try and find in the Dewey catalogue where he ought to be looking in the first place, then he looks in the subject index, finds the appropriate drawer and discovers that there are indeed two books on genetics in the library. But by the time he reaches the shelf, he finds that some other child who has not been anywhere near so conscientious has gone straight to the shelf and taken the books away. This is the problem, and indeed in the school where we worked, the librarian learnt from our survey and altered her own cataloguing system to make it much more readily accessible. She changed over to one of the metal-page systems in which you put strips of typed paper saying where books are located. She also used the very interesting expedient of having maps of the world and of Europe over the geography section, and labelling countries by name and by Dewey number. The reader had simply to look on the map of the world, read the Dewey number, and then could go to the shelf. This can make selection less mystifying.

Part of the problem is that most teachers were themselves fluent readers and were able to deduce what they ought to be doing in order to use books effectively. It is extremely difficult for us to realize that perhaps 90 per cent of the school population is not in the same position and will not spontaneously be able to work out what an index does, how it might be used, how the contents list at the beginning of a book might be used, what an appendix might be, how references might be used, how a bibliography might be used, and so on. I would suggest that these skills ought to be taught explicitly, and while the English department should most certainly be playing its part, it would be dangerous if I as a head of geography, for example, were to trust the English department to do it on their own. After all, are the research tasks they set going to be the same as the ones I might set?

Are the skills going to generalize from one curriculum area to another? We know very well that a child can do logarithms in mathematics lessons, but when he starts doing O-level physics and needs to do logarithms, the teacher often has to teach it all over again. It is very difficult to motivate children to use the skills they have acquired in one subject area in another subject, and it is important for every department to try to ensure that this is done in a co-ordinated way.

My final point is really a bridge between this section and the next. One of the questions we asked of teachers in our local authority visits on the reading project was what children needed to be able to do as far as using books was concerned. One of the points that came up most often was that they needed to be able to make effective notes. We asked the teachers how they taught children to make notes and unfortunately this question was very often answered by a rather embarrassed silence. If the teachers did describe any method at all it was one requiring the skills of both analysis and synthesis. In other words, the teacher gives children good notes which he has written himself, and from those notes the children may learn what it is to make effective notes. Of course, as soon as you look at this from the point of view of information processing, or from the point of view of the psychology of learning, it becomes clear that you could not really have a more complex and more demanding way of learning anything. It is vital that if children need to be able to take notes in your subject that you teach them how to do it. By all means demand and expect that the English department should be doing its bit. But précis and summary work with a vague and unspecified purpose in English is more difficult to teach, I would suggest, than note-making in history or geography where there is an explicit purpose for it. In such a case the child knows why it is important and can learn from you directly what it is to make the kind of judgement about the salience of names, dates, events or causes that is appropriate in your own subject area. This, then, is one issue that could be reflected on at department level and in departmental meetings.

Staff development

In thinking about learning as a department I would like to suggest one or two activities that the head of department might inject into a meeting in order to offer an opportunity for raising the level of awareness about reading. I have taken part in a number of exercises in which we have asked children to keep notes for one week on the reading demands that are being made of them. You ask a child to keep notes on what he has been reading in class and for homework, and perhaps what he has been writing as well, in each subject area. Over a week this generates a lot of useful information, and I have found on occasion that teachers have been shocked to be reminded just how difficult the demands are at fourth-year level, particularly when looking at homework reading.

The department might also look at the tasks that were associated with the reading material and ask why the children were required to read those particular sections, what they were supposed to be getting from their reading, and whether in fact they did gain from it.

I have suggested earlier that there could profitably be group decision-making about the selection of texts. This could imply, for example, a departmental visit to a local teachers' centre. If there is a university department of education or college education department nearby, you can guarantee that there will be a library of textbooks for your subject area, and it might be possible to visit that and have some input to inform a discussion on the possibilities of textbooks in your subject area.

Very often, as we all know, a publisher's representative arrives in the lunch-hour and you stand there, with a corned-beef sandwich in one hand and a book in another, trying to decide whether your department can afford it, and you are lucky if you can find one colleague to have a look at the book with you. These days, books cost so much that I think textbook adoption must become something towards which we develop a more professional attitude. A visit to the National Textbook Reference Collection (Taviton Street, London) might well be a useful in-service activity if it could be arranged. My point is that it is indefensible to spend £400 on a set of textbooks that perhaps only two colleagues have had a chance to look at, and which you have had no chance to pilot in the classroom.

Another exercise which can be done in a departmental meeting is to look at a cloze test of a passage taken from one of the textbooks used in the department. Every tenth word is deleted, and the reader's attempts to put in the missing words offer an interesting window into his understanding of the passage. They can also give you, as authors of classroom materials, an insight which you might not have had before into how much someone is (or is not) able to gain from the worksheets you have written.

I suggested earlier that year-group glossaries can be made

available to children and hung up in a classroom or laboratory. I think this is something which could profitably be discussed at departmental meeting level. After all, if there are key terms or key concepts in your own subject which you are wanting to reinforce through reading, then it is reasonable to ask in what order they should be introduced, and whether there is a structural development such that the ones you introduce in the second year follow on from the ones that were introduced in the first year, and so on. When you undertake this sort of exercise it soon becomes clear that the reading issue is a curriculum issue, and in talking about concepts that are introduced you could just as well be talking about curriculum structure as about reading problems: the two issues overlap at many points.

Developing children's reading

Finally, I want to focus again on the individual child, and to reiterate the point that motivation is crucial. A beautiful experiment by Shnayer[1] in the United States demonstrated that even comparatively poor readers, when they rated a passage as very interesting indeed, were able to perform on a comprehension test at the very same level as the most able readers. Although it does not happen too often, when someone is highly motivated they can read and comprehend at a level of performance well above their normal performance. However, it is clearly important to know something about the reading potential of a child, and here I would argue for wide dissemination of information about a child's reading ability, particularly when it could alert us to likely problems in handling print. I am thinking specifically of the vast amount of data that very often accompanies a child's move from junior to secondary school. Many schools go to a great deal of trouble to test children in the last two years of junior school and they have a fair amount of information about what that child can or cannot do as far as reading is concerned. Yet how many teachers in comprehensive schools have never looked at these records except in relation to matters of pastoral care? I would argue therefore that in departmental meetings this kind of information should be made available, or that if you have a first-year group you should seek the information out for yourself if it is available.

---

[1] S.W. Shnayer, 'Relationship between reading interest and reading education' in J. A. Figurel (ed.), *Reading and Realism*, Proceedings, vol. 13, Part I (1968), International Reading Association, Newark, Delaware.

The great majority of primary schools are wanting to do more than say that a child has a certain reading age on Schonell's Word Reading Test. They often offer a much more descriptive and helpful analysis than this, but until you try to find the information, you are hardly in a position to use it. I am aware of the danger of misusing test data and stigmatizing children as poor readers; my case is for the intelligent and sensitive use of such data in order to avoid a child's reaching the Easter of his first year in secondary school before anyone takes account of his reading problems.

In the classroom, I would not want to advocate a wholly individual approach to reading; I certainly feel there is plenty of room for whole-class discussion of a text. I would stress, however, that in most subjects homework can be an important problem. It is one thing to look at a difficult book in class when everyone is discussing it, but it is a totally different matter to have it set for homework. Of course, you cannot find a dozen different books according to the reading level of each child in the class. What is implied is an understanding of the difficulties a child might be encountering in taking a book home. As mentioned earlier, on the Effective Use of Reading Project we found that in general the harder a book was, the more likely it was for the child to be reading it independently, without the teacher's support. This came about because the most difficult texts were used in subjects such as science, history and geography, which had few periods per week and a heavy information load. On the project we came to feel that some teachers with low expectations of what children could gain from texts had helped to create their problem; only when they brought an attention to reading into their lessons would the children have an opportunity to learn how to cope with dense texts.

I have been fortunate to have had the chance to work with some very able teachers who have been developing reading through group work. We called it Silent Reading and Group Discussion (SRGD) and you may have come across the terms group cloze, group prediction, and group sequencing, which are three SRGD activities. In the final report of the Effective Use of Reading Project,[1] we say something about the exploratory work that was undertaken to evaluate SRGD. As an example we can consider the case of a teacher who used group sequencing to help with a familiar problem: children who could read perfectly adequately and yet would protest every time they encountered a worksheet, 'What have we got to do, Sir?'

[1] Eric Lunzer and Keith Gardner (eds), *The Effective Use of Reading*, op. cit.

A novel approach to this was adopted by a science teacher who was working part-time at Nottingham University on an M.Ed. He chopped up his worksheets into sections, then gave them to the children in random order with the instruction to work out what the correct order of the sections should be. They discussed it in groups, and he then told them whether or not they were right. They did this, and the teacher persuaded a colleague to keep a note of the number of times children came up to him and asked him what they had to do. He found they did not come. After they had done this little exercise, they had all worked out how to perform the experiment. The only questions he had were about the chemistry, not the instructions, while in a parallel class, using the same worksheet without an SRGD exercise, twenty-two children came up to ask questions about what to do.

What might have appeared to the children as a more or less amusing reading game was actually deadly serious. One of the problems in reading is getting children to operate on what they read rather than letting it just flow past their eyes. This was one way of doing that. Cloze procedure, in which a group of children look at a text which has words deleted at regular intervals, can also be very useful. If you get children doing cloze at the end of a period of work on a topic, or as a revision exercise, it can be very instructive for the children, but also for the teacher. For the less able there are ways of making print more accessible. Audio-visual approaches — tape-recordings with text attached to them — can be useful, but I think the real problem is matching the text to the child. If you can cope with this then you do not have the other problem of offering sound. As far as the more able reader is concerned, offering extra resources is crucial, and classroom libraries can be of immense value. I have seen some excellent ones in science, but not so many in other subject areas. In the best schools we visited on the reading project many departments had their own small library of teaching materials, and the heads of department had been able to purchase individual copies of other courses which were referred to by the staff.

I am conscious that in this brief chapter I have only been able to indicate the general directions work on reading might take. *The Effective Use of Reading* is a more extensive account of research, theory and practice in reading development, and its work has been extended in the Schools Council project Reading for Learning in the Secondary School (also based at Nottingham University). In another book, which Michael Marland edited, called *Language Across the*

Curriculum,[1] Keith Gardner and I make some points at greater length about the possible approaches to reading that can be adopted within a department, and these might be useful.

One of the most disturbing aspects of our research on the Effective Use of Reading Project was the discovery that many children were not being extended because teachers felt it was asking too much to expect them to work from dense texts. The result of this was that, particularly in the first three years of secondary schooling, children only encountered books rarely, and were unprepared for the heavy reading demands of CSE and GCE O-level courses. Caroline Burke,[2] the American researcher, has said that it is insane to deny a poor reader access to print. Our task must be to ensure that we make the appropriate demands so that children can learn to further their own reading and develop their own reading skills.

---

[1] Michael Marland (ed.), *Language Across the Curriculum: The Implementation of the Bullock Report in the Secondary School* (Heinemann Educational Books, 1977).

[2] In a paper delivered at UKRA Conference, 1977, Avery Hill College, London.

Postscript:
the art of the possible
Sydney Hill

A frequent and understandable reaction to courses attended and literature read about department management is 'That would not be possible to implement in my department or my school'. Understandable because the peculiarities of our own situations tend to place unique constraints on us, so that few paradigms of good practice or exhortations to take a particular course of action, however fervently we may agree with them, can be introduced as a neat package into the schools we know. Yet the very fact that we are conscious of these problems is, perhaps, a sign of the sort of awareness without which we would be less than qualified for departmental leadership.

However, it is palpably not the task of the course lecturer or writer on departmental management to be fettered by the very real concerns we all have. In the foregoing chapters, possible approaches to solving such dilemmas as intransigent staff and unsympathetic heads are, properly, touched on, but the very uniqueness of the constraints that in some mixture we all know precludes the possibility of such sources offering solutions. It seems to me that the major *raison d'être* of the chapters in this book is to present ideas which we can discuss, agree or disagree with, and adapt or reject, as appropriate. If our leadership is not to become fixed or passive, we need such touchstones.

Maurice Holt, Colin Bayne-Jardine, and others, point out and describe the ambiguities and complexities involved in departmental leadership, and Michael Marland (in Chapter 4) underlines how unaware so many candidates for promotion to such posts reveal themselves to be at interview. The caps we have to wear are many, as are those of colleagues to whom and for whom, in some aspects of their work, we are responsible. We may, as new heads of department, have the head or one of the deputies teaching our subject along with a head of year and even the head of another department. The problems of policy discussion, debate and implementation are heightened by such realities. Other calls on such teachers' time, thought and energy are many.

Responsibility for and to colleagues is, rightly, a recurrent theme in this book and what Peter Stokes calls 'the minefield of professional relationships' describes almost epigrammatically one of the most difficult tasks of management. As one of the green, newly appointed heads of department to whom Michael Marland refers, it was one of the most difficult aspects of my role. I think it was the encouraging words and occasional notes from the head in my early, hesitant weeks that indicated to me just how valuable such signs of interest and knowledge could be to members of my own team. It was a long time before I felt able to attempt the more difficult but none the less necessary task of giving frank and hopefully tactful criticism. Change that involves altering relationships with our colleagues is riddled with potential pitfalls and there is no short cut to changing the ethos and spirit of a department so that contact can be professional and frank as well as friendly. Conscious and determined yet gradual phasing of change that has repercussions on these relationships is crucial.

The multiplicity of tasks that so often contend for our attention can easily lead us to shelve considering and working on ideas we wish to adopt. Translating the ideal into the possible often involves compromise. What is possible is determined by resources, the most important of which are the energy, imagination and commitment of departmental staff and their ability to work together. Arguably, the most important task of the head of department is to create a climate that enables these resources to grow, be shared and used to serve the pupils.

The constant thinking through of current practice, conception of role and the consideration of new ideas that are necessary strands of effective leadership are what this book is intended to encourage.

Appendices

Appendix 1

Advice about administration

Coping with correspondence

1 Maintain an in-tray, supplemented by a 'pending' tray
2 Try to clear regularly, 'first in, first out'
3 Work through in-tray in whatever order it is in
4 Keep copies of key notes (try NCR[1] pads)
5 Send copies to relevant people, especially pastoral staff.

Meeting the needs of meetings

1 Have as few as possible
2 Have sufficient
3 Calendar at least a term in advance
4 Agenda efficiently, with few items
5 Ensure review of and preparation for main aspects in proper cycle
6 There are three main kinds: discussion, review, decision; be clear about purpose
7 Minute rapidly
8 Circulate agendas and minutes to senior staff as well as department
9 Start and end meetings very near indeed to announced timings
10 Act on decisions rapidly.

Points about paperwork

1 One item per sheet, except in bulletins
2 Copy to each person who needs to know, including those 'for information'
3 Specify action expected of each so that each knows what others are doing

[1] No carbon required.

4 Include circulation list
5 Name the recipient of each sheet: 'This copy for: ...'
6 File copies: sf, cf[1]
7 Use a bring-forward file[2]
8 In long documents, subdivide by logical structure, using indentations and headings
9 Write up immediately after meeting, interview, decision
10 Keep a few spare copies in a fixed place.

---

[1] 'sf' is 'subject file' — the copy filed under the heading of the subject; 'cf' is 'cumulative file' — the copy filed in consecutive date order.
[2] A dated file in which reminders for future action can be placed for 'bringing forward' for your attention.

Appendix 2

The head of department's role

(An outline from North Westminster Community School, London)

i *School leadership.* To contribute to the well-being and development of the school by supervision of pupils, guidance of teachers, and advice to the Director of Curriculum, various committees, and the Head. This responsibility is to be exercised by all Heads of Departments, both within and outside their actual departmental teams.

ii *Leadership of the team of teachers and ancillaries by:*
   (a) induction, guidance, and advice;
   (b) oversight of work of members of departments, including assessment and evaluation;
   (c) presenting the views of members of departments at, and reporting back from, all areas of consultation;
   (d) encouraging members of department to keep abreast of recent developments in subject areas;
   (e) assisting in the professional development of the teachers, including in-service work as may be appropriate, and career development;
   (f) discussing with the teachers about distribution of classes and recommendations to the Director of Curriculum;
   (g) advising the HM about recruiting, advertising, and appointing new staff.

iii *Responsibility structure* — to devise a suitable responsibility structure within the department, and to draw up suitable job specifications.

iv *Curriculum content* — responsibility for leading the department's curriculum planning, incorporating the whole-school policies; contributing relevant units or components to other departmental syllabuses as may be required.

v *Methodology* — responsibility for teaching approaches used within the subject team by development and selection of suitable materials, and by advising on classroom management appropriate to the relevant subject matter.

vi *Schemes of work* — responsibility for embodying (iv) and (v) in a full scheme of work to be made available to those who may require it.

vii *Liaison* — with Director of Curriculum, with Deputy Heads, Central Co-ordinators, Librarians, Media Research Officers, Heads of Houses, and other Heads of Department to ensure the best implementation of school and departmental policies by members of department and by visiting students.

viii *Accommodation and stock* — responsibility for departmental rooms, effective use of display and maintenance of good appearance; planning and wise spending of departmental allowances; and storage of and security for, equipment and software.

ix *Departmental records* — to be devised and maintained according to the school policy.

x *Teaching groups* — to allocate pupils to teaching groups within the department according to school and departmental policy, and to provide up-to-date staff lists.

xi *Discipline* — to accept responsibility for conduct and behaviour of pupils within the department and to be available to help members of department as problems arise.

xii *Information* — to provide information to parents and colleagues about the work of the department, and the progress of pupils.

xiii *Health and Safety Act* — to take any delegated responsibility for the implementation of the Act as may be agreed.

Appendix 3

The head of department's role

(A detailed description from Woodberry Down School, London)

A Head of Department is essentially a leader of his or her team of teachers, responsible to the Headmaster (normally via the Second Deputy) for the work of these teachers; the development of the subject, both its long-term planning and effective day-to-day teaching; for the care of staff and the articulation of their views; for the good working of pupils in that subject; for taking a major part (in conjunction with the Heads of House) in the evolving and implementation of school policy, and for the good order and pleasant atmosphere of the school.

A. Staff

1 The Head of Department's main responsibility is for the effectiveness of each member of his department, and he should observe each of his team at work in the classroom as often as possible.
2 Alerting the Headmaster of likely resignations as early as possible; liaising over replacements, *including drafting any necessary advertisements, and the job-description for applicants.* (It cannot be presumed that posts are always available for replacement.)
3 Advising Headmaster on selection of new staff, including short-listing, pre-interview visits, hospitality arrangements at interviews, and attending to question candidates and advise.
4 Liaison with newly appointed staff, including complete briefing, introduction to school and induction (in conjunction with Head of House and Senior Teacher: In-Service).
5 Guidance, assistance and training to staff as may be necessary.

6 Defining work of responsibility holders in the department and overseeing that the work is carried out.

7 Informing departmental staff fully of school policy, interpreting it to them, and ensuring that it is carried out.

8 Initiating and leading departmental discussion on school and subject matters, including at least two formal meetings a term, the minutes of which should be forwarded to the Second Deputy and HM.

9 Covering of absences by advance liaison with Second Deputy whenever possible, and making arrangements for the setting of work to supervised classes.

10 Ensuring that attendance registers and mark books are kept accurately.

11 Regular checking of the appropriate departmental teaching records, and sampling of written work.

12 Submitting detailed notes to HM towards probation forms, and, later, any testimonials.

13 Overseeing the work of departmental non-teaching staff, including checking hours as appropriate, in liaison with School Secretary who is nominally responsible.

14 Ensure that the School Secretary has addresses and telephone numbers of departmental staff, and that any changes are notified to him.

B. Pupils

1 The Head of Department is responsible, in the first instance, for the work and behaviour of all the pupils taught his or her subject whilst in the lessons of that subject.

2 Maintain adequate departmental records of each pupil taught by the department.

3 Where the subject is setted, place pupils in appropriate sets, *preparing lists for teachers in advance*, and supplying copies to Heads of Lower and Upper School as appropriate.

4 Ensure teachers keep Tutors informed of progress of pupils as appropriate.

5 Advise and assist teachers over individual pupils, taking disciplinary action where necessary, and making sure that Tutors or House staff are consulted over problems. (It is normally the Head of Department who is consulted by the Senior staff or House staff in the case of difficulties.)

6 Arrange for difficult pupils who may, e.g., need to be sent out of classes, and making sure this is known by department. (Pupils may not merely be left outside classroom doors.)

7 Supervise allocation of grades as required by school.

8 Advise pupils as necessary on choice of middle-school courses (in conjunction with House staff), sixth-form sub-

jects, and FE or HE (in conjunction with Senior Sixth-form Tutor).

9 Liaise with Head of Remedial Department over pupils needing special help.

C. Subject

1 Initiating subject discussion, ensuring that there is constant review of teaching approaches, consulting the Heads of schools, the Curriculum Co-ordinator, and the Headmaster throughout.

2 Prepare a complete working statement of the department's teaching method and content in a 'Scheme of Work', up-to-date copies of which should be given to the Headmaster, his three senior colleagues, and each House room.

3 Links with other departments where there are possibilities of links or co-operative work.

4 Establish strong links with the Remedial Department and with the Middle-School Support Option.

D. Parents

1 Inform parents of any points that affect their children in the subject *via Houses*.

2 Answer parents' letters or notes in pupils Diaries[1] where they refer to subject teaching, and ensure Tutor has copy of letter.

3 Advise staff on most effective ways of writing the school's reports to parents; check on completion and quality of entries.

4 Keep parents informed (by, e.g., circular letters, talks, exhibitions) of subject approach and of specific requirements from pupils.

E. Timetable

1 Review existing timetable with Curriculum Co-ordinator in late autumn/early January.

2 Advise ideas of the department for forthcoming year in broad terms in January/February.

3 Check curriculum details as issued by the Curriculum Co-ordinator during the spring.

4 Deduce staffing requirements, check against available staff, and notify credit/debit as far as possible to Second Deputy in late Spring.

5 Submit detailed lists of staffing suggestions (staff to classes

---

[1] At this school all pupils are issued with a school diary as a record of their teaching programme and homework assignments, and parents and tutors are expected to sign it weekly to indicate their satisfaction with the week's work.

and vice versa) after departmental discussion by summer half-term.

6 Check draft timetables as available.
7 Prepare basic rooms timetable.
8 Issue and explain timetable to staff.
9 Advise Curriculum Co-ordinator on any mid-year changes necessary.
10 Ensure that there are no unauthorised changes of time-table. NOTIFY ALL AGREED CHANGES IN WRITING.

F. School policy

1 Encourage discussion on school matters by department, and represent departmental teachers' views so that they can be taken into account.
2 Attend Heads of Departments' meetings (usually two per half-term). Submit matters for the agenda to the Head-master well in advance.
3 Interpret agreed policy to departmental staff, ensuring that they have full information, and that policy is carried out.

G. Accommodation and Equipment

1 Check maintenance of specialist accommodation with Schoolkeeper.
2 Order all departmental resources for learning, including books, slides, tapes, films; equipment, instruments and apparatus. (Liaise with Media Resources Officer, especially over audio-visual material.) Financial year runs from 1st September to 31st August. Liaise with School Sec-retary re correct exhausting of expenditure by means of Pass Book for each spending head for which Head of Department is responsible. Oversee local expenditure by department.
3 Liaise with Librarian, including the recommendation of books and other material, and the encouragement of staff to use the library with pupils.
4 Liaise with teacher i/c Bookshop.
5 Oversight of efficient stock control system, including security of equipment, detailed book checking system, and sending of bills for lost books. (Liaison with School Secretary over any losses and annual completion of stock book.) In case of losses by, *even suspected*, burglary or theft, it is vital to inform the Schoolkeeper *at once* (not, say, after the lapse of a weekend).
6 Advise the Headmaster of budget needs for the following year when asked.

7 Oversee the submission of material for duplicating, etc. (See Standing Instructions — Reprographics sheet.)
8 *Furniture keys*: ensure all staff understand procedure, and draw and hold keys for furniture serving *departmental* (as distinct from Tutorial) purposes. Head of Department to draw from School Secretary, and hold available for emergencies, a duplicate set of these departmental keys.

H. *Examinations*

1 Arrange for setting, duplication of papers by office (submit well in advance), collation, and delivery of all internal examinations.
2 Check examination timetables.
3 *Personally* or by *direct delegation to a senior colleague* inform pupils of external examination entry decisions.
4 Head of Department is responsible for informing Examinations Administrator of accurate and up-to-date information on examinations in their subject: accurate entry lists, changes of examination policy, new boards and new modes, etc.

I. *Students*

1 Ensuring departments have a consistent and understood policy.
2 Establishing links with training institutions agreed with Senior Teacher: In-Service, who has overall responsibility for students.
3 Agreeing with Senior Teacher: In-Service the numbers to accept in coming year.
4 Planning timetables in advance, receiving students for preliminary visit, preparing documentation.
5 Supervising phased induction of students, and deciding cautiously when each may work without a teacher colleague in room.
6 Organising departmental seminars as advisable.
7 Preparing reports for Senior Teacher: In-Service for training institutions.

J. *Records*

1 Keep clear records of decisions, meetings, interviews and correspondence.
2 Prepare detailed briefing notes for successor, and be prepared for phased hand-over.

Appendix 4

Job specification within a department
(Woodberry Down School English department responsibilities)

Head of Department

1 *Ultimate responsibility* for all departmental policy decisions, the implementation of these, classroom practice, and other departmental activities.

2 *Responsibility for pupil progress, welfare and discipline* within the department and devising and maintenance of adequate records of these.

3 *Professional welfare of department staff*: Ensuring active and relevant participation of staff in pupils' welfare and departmental organisation, to enhance prospects of promotion through the development of professional skills and knowledge of as many aspects of teaching and administration as possible. Encouragement of in-service training.

4 *Timetabling* of staff to teaching groups, encouraging as fair and comprehensive a spread of work as possible.

5 *Internal and external examination policy and administration*: With the Second in Charge.

6 *Requisition, issue and care of stock*: In consultation with other members of department.

7 *Permission* for visits in and out, staff absences, courses and communications out to parents and others.

8 *Heads of department meetings*: Attendance at and reporting back to department and acting on decisions taken.

9 *Department documentation*: Devising and care of. Permission for any circulars and publications.

10 *Fourth- and fifth-year English*: Responsibility for policy, working, modification, duplication and distribution of syllabuses. Suggesting and checking stock. Convening meetings of teachers. Availability and filing of up-to-date

set lists. Collection from staff and checking of reports prior to sending to office.

11 *A-level*: Overall responsibility for syllabus, teaching, group composition and examination entry.

12 *Stock list*: Distribution of up-to-date lists of stock and specifying use of stock.

13 *Students*: Welfare and timetabling of students attached to the department.

14 *IBM*: Links between IBM and the department.

Joint Second-in-Charge

1 *Deputising* for and *liaising* with the Head of Department in the event of his absence or other commitments.

2 *Policy and practice*: Discussing and monitoring with the Head of Department the theoretic basis of the department's work and the effectiveness of its teaching within this framework, this to include any necessary production maintenance and up-dating of department documentation.

3 *First-year English*: Responsibility for policy, working, modification, duplication and distribution of syllabuses. Suggesting and checking stock. Convening meetings of first-year English teachers. Availability and filing of up-to-date set lists. Collection from staff and checking of reports prior to sending to office.

4 *CSE Examinations*: Administration and organisation of these with the Head of Department, including production of accurate entry lists and filing of duplicate mark sheets and other information.

5 *English-Library liaison*: Responsibility for library skills policy and working in accordance with library curriculum document. Encouraging use and complementary stocking.

6 *Bookshop*: Responsibility for oversight and organisation in liaison with person in charge. Policy for use by the department.

7 *Primary—secondary English*: Establishment of links with primary schools towards relevant foundation-year course at Woodberry Down.

Joint Second-in-Charge

1 *Deputising* for and *liaising* with the Head of Department in the event of his absence or other commitment.

2 *Policy and practice*. Discussing and monitoring with the Head of Department the theoretic basis of the department's work and the effectiveness of its teaching within this framework, this to include any necessary produc-

tion maintenance and up-dating of department documentation.
3 *Third-year English*: Responsibility for policy, working,
modification, duplication and distribution of syllabuses.
Suggesting and checking stock. Convening meetings of
third-year English teachers. Availability and filing of up-to-
date set lists. Collection from staff and checking of reports
prior to sending to office. Examination administration.
4 *GCE O-level examinations*: Administration and organising
of these with the Head of Department, including production
of accurate entry lists and filing of duplicate mark sheets
and other information.
5 *Department publications*: Initiating and overseeing of any
magazines or broadsheets issued by the department.
6 *Courses and meetings*: Notification of these to the department. Liaison with English Centre and Teachers' Centres.

Third-in-Charge

1 *Upper school non-A-level English*: Arranging and administration of internal and external examinations. Decision on
those to take O-level language from within CEE groups.
Liaison with the Head of Department, tutors and houses
over progress and problems. Suggesting and checking
stock. Availability and filing of up-to-date set lists. Collection from staff and checking of reports prior to sending
to office.
2 *Second-year English*: Responsibility for policy, working,
modification, duplication and distribution of syllabuses.
Suggesting and checking stock. Convening meetings of
second-year English teachers. Availability and filing of
up-to-date set lists. Collection from staff and checking of
reports prior to sending to office.
3 *Book boxes*: Administration, stock suggestions and distribution.
4 *Filing and renewing of worksheets*: Ensuring that staff can
quickly locate material desired and have an easy reference
system of all worksheets in stock. One copy of every
sheet produced to be lodged with her. Decisions on what
to be kept.
5 *Minuting of departmental meetings*.

Teacher

1 *Audio-visual hardware and software*: Provision and maintenance of these within the department. Liaison with
MRO and teacher in charge of Film Studies, distribution

of lists of information on stock. Labelling and storage. Maintenance of an up-to-date stock list.

2 *Consumable stock*: Ordering, storage and issue of consumable stock. Keeping of up-to-date record of orders and spending.

3 *Stock in Room 23*: Recording, care of and issuing of stock.

4 *Reading Centre*: responsibility for theory and practice timetabling of staff and pupils, liaison with Head of English, Head of Lower School, houses, tutors and others as appropriate.

Teacher

1 *Reports*: Collection of slips from member of staff responsible for a particular year, and filing of these.

2 *Department reference stock*: Maintenance, recording and checking.

3 *Records of work*: Distribution, collection and filing of half-termly sheets. Organising collection and filing of a piece of writing per pupil per year.

Appendix 5

Attitudes and skills: an example from a humanities scheme of work

V. *Attitudes*

V.0 The syllabuses of the Humanities Department should individually and severally encourage the pupils to:

V.1 develop an interest in other people, events and things, which will include:
   (a) curiosity
   (b) speculation
   (c) the ability to see connections

V.2 develop an awareness to:
   (a) new ideas
   (b) other ways of seeing
   (c) different life-styles

V.3 develop an imaginative understanding of:
   (a) other eras
   (b) other places
   (c) other people
   (d) other beliefs
   so as to encourage:
      (i) tolerance
      (ii) sympathy
      (iii) generosity

V.4 value:
   (a) other individuals for themselves
   (b) the whole spectrum of human achievements
   (c) their own personal qualities and potential and the quality of their own work
   (d) the natural and the built environments

V.5 judge critically, including to:
    (a) analyse
    (b) assess evidence accurately and objectively (i.e. with honesty and due impartiality as far as possible given the limitations of data and the judge's social and cultural position)
    (c) hypothesise
    (d) draw conclusions rationally
    (e) acquire a sense of flexibility, which, in turn, might lead to a change in stance.

VI. *Skills*

VI.0 All the work in the Humanities should aim to develop the following skills or abilities at all levels:

VI.1 *Evidence*
To be able to seek out and make appropriate use of evidence:
    (a) to be able to search for and find evidence:
        (i) in the library
        (ii) in the street and landscape: looking within the environment and its materials
        (iii) in museums
        (iv) through the oral tradition, from people themselves, listening to what people have to say and recollect
    (b) to be able to 'read' evidence (to read critically, 'between the lines and beyond the lines'), from
        (i) reference or broken prose
        (ii) continuous prose
        (iii) original documents, manuscripts, forms, maps, diagrams, photographs, film, TV, art works, cartoons, tables of statistics, graphs
        (iv) natural scenes, natural objects, artefacts, the built environment

    Reading skills involve observations, understanding standard printed symbols and conventions, and having background knowledge.
    (c) to be able to collect, record and organise evidence:
        (i) make notes
        (ii) interview
        (iii) write
        (iv) use the telephone
        (v) make audio recordings

        (vi) photograph
      (vii) sketch
   (viii) prepare drawings with notes
 (d) to be able to evaluate:
        (i) to be able to sift and sort the evidence and materials collected
      (ii) to develop the critical faculties, including to be able to test bias within the sources
   (iii) to be able to select, juxtapose and re-compose the evidence, which involves selecting parts, selecting different sources, seeing connections, and drawing conclusions
 (e) to be able to organise the accumulation of evidence, including by:
        (i) maintaining folders or files
      (ii) sorting and arranging gathered material
   (iii) indexing and labelling as appropriate
 (f) to have sense of appropriate accuracy.

VI.2 *Memory*
To be able to memorise such facts as will be useful.

VI.3 *Generalisation*
To be able to draw the appropriate generalisation.

VI.4 *Presentation*
To be able to present one's own knowledge or ideas:
 (a) in writing:
        (i) various short answers
      (ii) continuous prose
 (b) visually:
        (i) diagrams
      (ii) maps
   (iii) drawings
   (iv) graphs
    (v) photo's, slides, film or video
 (c) orally:
        (i) in discussion
      (ii) in talks and 'presentations'
   (iii) on tape.

Appendix 6

From a description of a language liaison policy across a community of schools

The language of reading

	Typographical Devices	The Parts of Books	The Aspects of a Library	Reading and Study Skills
Infant	initial initials	book page cover	left—right sequencing of numbers and of letters	letter word sentence
Lower Junior	italics bold margin (= the space, not the line)	title author chapter index (basic) cover: spine, jacket	reference (= cannot be taken from library) dictionary encyclopaedia	fact, non-fiction fiction opinion main idea paragraph
Upper Junior	asterisks column Roman numeral guide words	section subsection diagram text illustration list of illustrations list of contents	volume (= a separately bound part of a large book) catalogue (= a list arranged in one form or another of all the books held)	conclusion dialogue quotation guide-words (= the word at head of page for identification)

	index (more detail) title page glossary introduction publisher printer end-paper	classify/classification	bibliography and further reading 'see' and 'see also' argument evidence context
Lower Secondary symbol	publication date chapter headings tables SBN editor frontispiece	catalogue: index to catalogue classified Dewey Decimal Classification (title only, plus 'General')	
Upper Secondary	introduction: preface foreword introduction addenda errata corrigenda footnotes edition/impression appendices half title fly leaf	periodical issue (= a particular periodical issue) Dewey in greater detail	hypothesis example premise skim scan

Further reading

Language in learning

BARNES, D., et al. *Language, the Learner and the School*. Harmondsworth: Penguin Books, 1971.

BRENNAN, W. K. *Reading for Slow Learners: A Curriculum Guide*. Schools Council Curriculum Bulletin 7. Evans/Methuen Educational, 1978.

HEALY, M. and MARLAND, M. *Language Across the Curriculum*. An exhibition catalogue, National Book League, 1980.

LUNZER, E. and GARDNER, K. (eds). *The Effective Use of Reading*. Heinemann Educational Books for the Schools Council, 1979.

MARLAND, M. (ed.). *Language Across the Curriculum: The Implementation of the Bullock Report in the Secondary School*. Heinemann Educational Books, 1977.

MARTIN, N. (ed.). *Writing and Learning Across the Curriculum 11—16*. Ward Lock Educational, 1976.

SELF, D. *Talk: A Practical Guide to Oral Work in the Secondary School*. Ward Lock Educational, 1976.

WILKINSON, A., STRATTA, L. and DUDLEY, P. *The Quality of Listening*. Schools Council Research Studies. Basingstoke: Macmillan Education, 1974.

Assessment and testing

DEALE, R. N. *Assessment and Testing in the Secondary School*. Schools Council Examinations Bulletin 32. Evans/Methuen Educational, 1976.

LEWIS, D. G. *Assessment in Education*. University of London Press[1], 1974. Probably the most accessible introduction to theoretical aspects, it is also practically based and useful for this too. Good on standardized tests.

MACINTOSH, H. G. (ed.) *Techniques and Problems of Assessment*. Edward Arnold, 1974.

SHIPMAN, M. *In-School Evaluation*. Heinemann Educational Books, 1979. First rate.

THORNDIKE, R. L. and HAGEN, E. P. *Measurement and Evaluation in Psychology and Education*. New York: John Wiley, 1969. An Ameri-

[1] Now Hodder & Stoughton Educational, Dunton Green.

can publication: encyclopaedic and particularly useful on objective testing and aspects of personality assessment. Weak on orals and practicals.

VERNON, P. E. *The Measurement of Abilities.* University of London Press[1], 1972.

Library research and study skills

BESWICK, N. *Resource-based Learning.* Heinemann Educational Books, 1977.

BRAKE, T. *The Need to Know.* British Library Research and Development Department Report no. 5511. British Library Research and Development Department, 1980.

DAVIES, R. A. *The School Library Media Center: A Force for Educational Excellence.* 2nd edn. Ann Arbor: Bowker, 1974.

GIBBS, G. *Learning to Study: A Guide to Running Group Sessions.* Milton Keynes: Institute for Educational Technology, The Open University, 1977.

IRVING, A. 'Teach them to learn'. *Educational Libraries Bulletin,* vol. 21 (2), (Summer 1978), pp. 29—39.

IRVING, A. and SNAPE, W. H. *Educating Library Users in Secondary Schools.* British Library Research and Development Department, 1979.

KAMM, A. and TAYLOR, B. *Books and the Teacher.* University of London Press[1], 1966.

LONGWORTH, N. ' "Information" in secondary-school curricula'. M.Phil. thesis, Southampton University, 1976.

LUBANS, J. *Educating the Library User.* Ann Arbor: Bowker, 1974.

LUNZER, E. and GARDNER, K. (eds). *The Effective Use of Reading.* Heinemann Educational Books for the Schools Council, 1979.

MARLAND, M. (ed.). *Language Across the Curriculum: The Implementation of the Bullock Report in the Secondary School.* Heinemann Educational Books, 1977.

ROE, E. *Teachers, Librarians and Children.* St Albans: Crosby Lockwood, 1965.

SMITH, M. J. and WINKWORTH, F. *Library-user Education: A Bibliography of Teaching Materials for Schools and Colleges of Further Education.* British Library Research and Development Department Report no. 5436. British Library Research and Development Department, 1978.

WINKWORTH, F. *User Education in Schools: A Survey of the Literature on Education for Library and Information Use in Schools.* British Library Research and Development Report no. 5391. British Library Research and Development Department, 1977.

---

[1] Now Hodder & Stoughton Educational, Dunton Green.

Notes on contributors

COLIN BAYNE-JARDINE was Headmaster of Culverhay School, Bath, for six years prior to taking up his present post as Headmaster of Henbury School, Bristol in 1976, and has also taught in the USA, Canada, Glasgow and Devonshire. As well as volumes on Mussolini and the Second World War, he has written about the study and teaching of history.

RORY DEALE has taught in independent, secondary modern, grammar and comprehensive schools, and for five years prior to taking up his present post as Assistant Education Officer (Curriculum Development) with Suffolk County Council in 1976, he was a member of the Schools Council Central Examinations Research and Development Unit. His publications include Schools Council Examinations Bulletin 32, *Assessment and Testing in the Secondary School* (Evans/Methuen Educational, 1976), Schools Council Examinations Bulletin 37 (joint author with Leslie Cohen), *Assessment by Teachers in Examinations at 16+* (Evans/Methuen Educational, 1977), and a chapter on assessment in *Mixed Ability Teaching*, ed. Brian Davies and Ronald G. Cave (Ward Lock Educational, 1977).

COLIN HARRISON taught English in grammar and comprehensive schools before joining the team of the Schools Council Effective Use of Reading Project (1973—76). He wrote and presented the BBC radio series, *Reading After Ten*, and was consultant for the BBC Schools Television series, *A Good Read*. He is co-editor of the *Journal of Research in Reading* and author of *Readability in the Classroom* (Cambridge University Press, 1980). He is currently a lecturer in the School of Education at Nottingham University.

SYDNEY HILL is Senior Teacher: Curriculum Development at Christopher Wren School, London, and was previously Head of English and Chairman of the Language Across the Curriculum Working Party at Woodberry Down School. He previously taught at The Lymm Grammar School, Cheshire, and The Cherwell School, Oxford.

MAURICE HOLT is Professional Studies Leader, College of St. Mark and St. John, Devon. Prior to setting up an Education and Curriculum Consultancy in 1977, he was the first Headmaster of Sheredes School in

Hertfordshire, a purpose-built mixed school where he was instrumental in organizing a common curriculum within a non-streamed format, featuring a faculty structure and block timetabling. He is the author of *The Common Curriculum* (Routledge & Kegan Paul, 1978).

ANN IRVING is a chartered librarian, who has worked in public, children's, school and college of education libraries. She has researched several projects with the British Library Research and Development Department and is now a lecturer and liaison and training officer in the Department of Library and Information Studies at Loughborough University. She is joint author of *Educating Library Users in Secondary Schools* with W. H. Snape (British Library Research and Development Department, Report no. 5467, 1979).

MICHAEL MARLAND, before becoming Headmaster of the Inner London Education Authority's first 'federal' comprehensive school, North Westminster Community School, in January 1980, was Headmaster of Woodberry Down School, London, for nine years. Prior to that, most of his teaching experience was in large London comprehensive schools. He was a member of the Bullock Committee, and is Chairman of the Schools Council English Committee and the National Book League's Use of Books in Schools Working Party. As well as being a frequent broadcaster and lecturer on a wide range of educational issues, he is general editor of the Heinemann Organization in Schools Series. His numerous publications include *Language Across the Curriculum: The Implementation of the Bullock Report in the Secondary School* (Heinemann Educational Books, 1977), and *Head of Department* (Heinemann Educational Books, 1971). He was awarded the CBE for services to education in the Queen's Silver Jubilee Honours List and made Honorary Professor of Education at Warwick University in 1980.

GEORGE PHIPSON, before becoming Deputy Head responsible for curriculum and timetabling at Abbey Wood School, London, was Head of Mathematics and Senior Teacher: In-Service Training at Woodberry Down School, and a teacher of mathematics at Bristol Grammar School. As well as lecturing on timetabling, he has contributed to the forthcoming book *School-Focussed In-Service Training* to be edited by Ray Bolam and published by Heinemann Educational Books.

PETER STOKES spent fifteen years teaching in technical high, bilateral, secondary modern and comprehensive schools, holding posts including head of department and headmaster. He has been a chief examiner for history with GCE and CSE boards and spent a year seconded to the Cayman Islands Government organizing their high school system. He is now Chief Adviser of Schools for the London Borough of Havering.

Index